INFINITY AND BEYOND

INFINITY and BEYOND

A Love Story Without End

Lynette Leitch

Canaan Press

First printed in Great Britain in 2005 by
Canaan Press - the book imprint of

Contact :
12 The Hard
PO22 6JS
lyneHe leitch@mac.com

British Library Cataloguing in Publication Data
A record for this book is available from the British Library

ISBN: 0-9551816-0-7
        978-0-9551816-0-3

Scripture taken from The Message by Eugene H. Peterson,
copyright © 1993, 1994, 1995, 1996, 2000, 2001, 2002. Used
by permission of NavPress Publishing Group. All rights
reserved.

Cover design by Tobias Outerwear for Books
www.tobiasdesign.com
from original photographs by Mark and Lynette Leitch

Manufactured in Malta by Gutenberg Press Limited

All for love...

This could only be for my son Matthew,

I thank God for your life, your courage, your inspiration and the joy of being your mum. I love you Matt, infinity and beyond...

and for my husband Mark,

for better, for worse, for richer, for poorer, in sickness and in health...I'm lost without you.

and for Matt's friends

Robbie, Simon, Jack, Ross, Fahad, Adil, Callum, Luke, Tom, Simon, Kyle

"Love one another the way I have loved you.
This is the very best way to love.
Put your life on the line for your friends."

John 15:12 -13 The Message

So many people have encouraged us to carry on in the face of trials, and given of their time and talents and prayers to help complete this book, please know that although your names are not listed here they are etched on our hearts.

Matthew Leitch – History Maker
30.12.1988 – 24.11.2002

"I'm gonna be a history maker in this land
I'm gonna be a speaker of truth to all mankind
I'm gonna stand
I'm gonna run
Into your arms
Well it's true today,
that when people stand with the fire of God,
and the truth in hand
We'll see miracles
we'll see angels sing
we'll see broken hearts making history.
Yes it's true and I believe it,
we're living for You."

(Martin Smith © 1996 Curious Music UK)

This book is absolutely compelling. It's a real life story of a mum and dad's agony at losing their only son. The real heros in life are those that find grace in the darkest places, here you will find two extraordinary examples of this.

Martin Smith, Singer/Songwriter – Deliriou5?

This book will strike a chord with every parent – a compelling account and a wonderful tribute to a remarkable young man and a love that knows no bounds.

Jane – mother of Sebastian Gates 1994-2003

Most often we travel life oblivious of the pain others live with, then sometimes we are drawn a little closer and are desperately grateful that it is not us, and then for some it becomes us.

There are opportunities in this life which we will never have in heaven. One of those, and I believe the most intense, is to choose to worship God in the midst of pain, loss and sadness. Lynette and Mark made that choice in the midst of the greatest loss, deepest grief and most inexplicable of circumstances. This book tells why they were able to do that as their lives were turned from the ordinary to the extraordinary and despite the absence of a miraculous healing, embrace our extraordinary God.

Paul Manwaring, Pastor – Bethel Church, Redding, CA.

Does all this work? Part way through chemotherapy I thought perhaps I was wasting my time. I lost the drive and enthusiasm for the change of lifestyle and chucked the diet suggestions out of the window. Never had I felt so ill during treatment!

It is two and a half years since I was diagnosed with cancer, I have been through all my chosen treatment and now live a very active, normal life. My daughter and I had the privilege of finally meeting Mark and Lynette at Matt's Canaan Retreat and discovered the peaceful haven from where so much love and help flows for people like myself.

Laura Canning – Breast cancer survivor

Nutrition and exercise play an important role in well-being but it is love and understanding of the patient beyond the physical that will enable us to make profound differences in the healing of diseases. If modern medicine is to succeed then the time has come to universally address more than just the physical body. Lynette and Mark gave up everything to be by Matt's side. He lives on through them to extend their important message to others.

Ko (Kauser) Chohan, Co-Author of Best-Selling 'Detox for Life'

"Unless a grain of wheat is buried in the ground,
dead to the world,
it is never any more
than a grain of wheat.

But if it is buried, it sprouts
and reproduces itself many times over.
In the same way,
anyone who holds on to life just as it is
destroys that life.
But if you let it go,
reckless in your love,
you'll have it forever,
real and eternal."

John 12:24
The Message

A Word Before...

The blistering heat of the afternoon sun burned down on the stones of the drive outside. But in my thick-walled fortress welcome shade cooled the desk where I sat. There was little breeze despite the tall open farmhouse windows and the air had that dry, parched-earth smell about it. The lanky stalks of maize in the field opposite stood like lofty sentinels guarding my hideaway.

How odd it seemed to be here. A wave of nostalgia flooded my being, drowning me in loneliness. We had left our son, our family and our friends in England all because of a dream to make a difference and honour the memory of an exceptional boy.

Struggling to see through tears, I typed on. Our story had brought us here to south west France where the sunshine warmed my skin but a desolate feeling chilled my soul. Would I discover a freedom in my spirit or remain a prisoner in this place? Would the vision we birthed in the cold English winter blossom and bear fruit in these warmer climes or would it wither and die, leaving only the dried up husk of a seed?

Chapter 1

The saying *'we all enjoy 20/20 vision with hindsight'* is a seductive phrase. It lures us into thinking that we might have altered the course of our lives if we knew then what we know now. But of course, life is not like that, even though it is littered with choices, we cannot press a rewind button and do it again. And we only torment ourselves to even consider the possibility. But surely what hindsight can allow us to do is use the knowledge and experience we have gained from past decisions to help others? I'd like to think so.

It was only after our son had been ill for some time that parts of a complicated jigsaw began falling into place. Whether or not hindsight would have altered the final outcome we shall never know this side of heaven, but it would most certainly have affected some life-changing decisions we made. And that hindsight used effectively now can hopefully make a difference in many other lives.

To take you back to the beginning, or rather the beginning of what now seems like a surreal dream, April 26th 2001 panned out like many other days in ordinary family life, if there is such a state.

It was a Thursday, and for our son Matthew, then twelve, that meant a school day. Living in one town in Berkshire and attending middle school in another, due to a recent house move, Matt had to be driven the slow and busy route to school every day. We had entertained friends for a birthday dinner the previous evening and they had stayed overnight. As part of the celebrations my husband, Mark, was due to play golf the next morning and I remember him offering to give me a break and drop Matt off at school on the way to the course. Bed was welcoming and warm that chilly April day and so I snuggled down for an extra few minutes and called out to our son as he left that I loved him and would see him later.

"Love you too, Mum," came his characteristic reply as he poked his head around our bedroom door before disappearing down the stairs. I too looked forward to a welcome treat that day as I was to go shopping with a girlfriend. Our time together passed pleasantly; women bond so well shopping. Congested traffic on our return prevented me from collecting Matthew from school and so my husband picked him up on his way home.

Other friends were visiting that evening, prior to emigrating to America, and the time before they arrived passed quickly amidst the usual post-school activities. When they arrived, Matt went outside to hang out with their son and Mark and I spent most of the evening discussing our friends' complete change of lifestyle. I recall saying, "Compared to you, our lives seem rather ordinary."

Regretfully, I cannot actually remember having any real conversation with Matt that day, mainly because our paths had not crossed much and as a typical twelve year old, although we were a close family, he usually preferred the company of his peers to 'dull old parents'.

Mark spoke to him shortly before nine o'clock and then joined us to say that Matt had complained of a headache. He'd asked his dad to pray for him, something our family does before reaching for medicines and had gone up to bed, leaving his friend at the computer. That was the last time either of us saw Matthew completely well. Within ten hours he was gravely ill in intensive care, cause unknown.

After our friends left, the remainder of that night passed in a frightening blur. It was late as we wearily headed upstairs for bed. I began to get undressed while Mark peeked into Matt's room to check, as we always did, that he was all right. He heard Matthew murmuring quietly, it sounded like he still had a headache and came to tell me. I got some liquid pain relief and went to see if there was anything I could do for my son. He was lying in his favourite position, on his tummy with his face turned sideways towards the wall, on the top of his newly-acquired sofa-cum-bunk bed. It was difficult to reach him to give him the medicine and I asked him to turn over. He seemed unable to comply with my request and his behaviour and the sounds he made were strangely worrying.

Feeling oddly uncomfortable and a little alarmed, I called Mark back into the room. With difficulty he looked at Matthew and then at me and we silently decided we needed to get him down to where we could better examine and help him. As I climbed up the uncomfortable metal steps and onto the bed, Matt still seemed unable to move. I lifted him up which was no mean feat, as he was a big guy for his age. I was alarmed to see that his face looked strange. The whole of the left-hand side was distorted. His mouth was drooping and his left eyelid was half closed. With great difficulty, and I'm sure discomfort for Matt, we managed to lift him down from the bunk with Mark somehow supporting him, and half carrying him into our room we laid him on our bed.

As we examined more closely fear shot through my body. I felt sick. Matthew seemed to be trying to smile, but the smile resembled that of someone who has suffered a stroke, and both his eyes were looking unnaturally up to one side and flickering. I remember both of us talking to him, asking simple questions like, "Can you see us"... hear

3

us... follow a finger?" It did not seem as if he could. With alarm rising, Mark picked up the telephone and dialled the emergency doctor's switchboard.

Chapter 2

We waited, really concerned...still trying to communicate with Matthew. Very soon the phone rang. It was the emergency doctor saying that she was unable to come to our house immediately and in view of our brief appraisal of the situation we should call an ambulance. We did. We also made another call to a member of our church. They operate a twenty four hour prayer chain and if anyone needs prayer for anything, they can call anytime, day or night, and that request would filter along a chain of willing volunteers who would immediately comply. It felt very comforting to do that.

We waited, silently praying...trying not to panic. The ambulance arrived promptly and two medics spent the next fifteen or twenty minutes examining Matthew and asking questions. It was obvious that something was very wrong, for as well as the changes to Matt's face, he seemed paralysed down his left-hand side and was unable to speak properly. He couldn't coordinate his movements and kept losing his balance as if he was going to fall off the bed.

We waited, confused...After what seemed an eternity, but was in fact only a short time, the medics decided that they could not say what was wrong with our son, but intuitively knew he would need a brain scan. The nearest hospital's scanner was out of action that day, so they decided to drive the extra distance to the Accident and Emergency Department in Wexham Park Hospital near Slough, about half an hour's drive away at that time of night.

It was arranged that I should accompany Matthew in the ambulance and Mark, seeming calmer and more able to drive, would follow in our car. I quickly got dressed and grabbed a sweater, my handbag and Bible, as the medics lifted Matt into the carrying-chair and strapped him in. Suddenly and without warning, as they tilted him back to lift him, he was violently sick. It was projectile and profuse.

We cleaned him up and hurriedly transferred him to the ambulance, sensing that time was of the essence. Matthew was strapped firmly onto the stretcher in preparation for the journey and I joined a medic sitting alongside him. The other medic climbed into the driver's seat instructing Mark to follow but to obey the speed limit. If they needed to accelerate Matt's journey to the hospital they were authorised to speed, but Mark was not.

I remember feeling so scared that I felt sick deep in my stomach. After we had been travelling for about ten minutes Matt suddenly started having a seizure, initially in his face, then all down one side. At the time I had no real concept of what was happening to him, I just knew I didn't like it. To calm myself and do the only thing I could, I began to pray out loud. As the seizure became more violent, affecting his entire body, the medic unstrapped him, and shouting to the driver to pull in, he started to administer a suppository drug to Matthew to control the fitting.

The ambulance came to a hasty stop and the driver climbed through to assist. Minutes later Mark pulled up behind us in the lay-by, but the medics would not allow me to let him inside the ambulance and concentrated all their attention on trying to arrest the seizure. The whole experience was beyond anything I had lived through and I could only focus on Matthew's distorted expression and violently shaking body. I could see Mark's concerned face peering through the back window. With tears filling my eyes, I pressed my open hand on the inside of the window pane and mouthed "I love you."

After being given the maximum dose of sedatives allowed by the medics, Mattie was still seizing violently. His body was racked, and the sounds coming from his throat tore at my heart. My son's condition was obviously serious but I was powerless to help him. To allay the mounting panic I felt, I prayed harder and louder. I recall wondering if my son was having an epileptic fit and thinking that it may affect him obtaining a driving licence when he was older. What bizarre thoughts form in our troubled minds!

Climbing back into his seat, the driver announced he would head for the hospital at top speed and we were to hang on. The rest of the journey seemed endless, but we eventually stopped outside the A&E doors and were met by several rushing figures. Expeditely, Matthew's stretcher disappeared into the hospital as Mark arrived. Seeing his pained expression I waited for him and grabbed his hand tightly as we followed our son into the glaring lights of the hospital corridor.

It was after midnight – another day had begun.

Chapter 3

As a family, we had all more or less enjoyed good health. Apart from the usual seasonal colds, occasional trips to the doctor's and rare visits for treatment of minor injuries as Matt adventurously explored life, hospitals were not commonplace for us. I don't remember taking in much of our surroundings that night, my attention was focused microscopically on one thing only – my son's body transferred to the stationary bed in the emergency room. After some time, still unable to arrest the seizure, the doctor informed us that he would need to administer stronger medication to Matt and would therefore need to place a tube down his throat to assist his breathing as the drugs could suppress his respiratory system.

Mark and I stood motionless, holding our breath as tubes were put down Matthew's throat and he was attached to a machine that did his breathing for him. The fear I felt was asphyxiating as I stood trying to take in all that was happening. I kept praying inside my head, I kept squeezing Mark's hand and I kept looking at my now unconscious son in disbelief. I called our prayer contact, updating them, listened to words of encouragement and felt comforted that people cared enough to get up in the middle of the night and pray for us.

We followed Matthew into further unknown territory as he was wheeled out to have a CT scan – that is a series of detailed pictures of the brain created by a computer linked to an x-ray machine. Fairly soon afterwards, the doctor in charge that night came to tell us that the scan had detected a shadow in the frontal lobe area of Matthew's brain and they would be transferring him as soon as possible to the Radcliffe Infirmary in Oxford, where specialists would examine Matt and best advise on his condition and treatment.

My knowledge of hospital jargon and activity was more or less restricted to overly-dramatic television programmes, so I tried not to be too anxious, and pushing down questions I had no desire to have answered, I held onto Mark dreamlike as we followed Matt's bed into the Intensive Care Unit to await his transfer.

By six that morning, we were in our car, following the ambulance that carried our precious son to yet another strange environment. While Mark drove, I made calls on the mobile to close friends, asking them to inform our families and take care of any urgent matters. On the surface I was keeping busy, but underneath feeling numb, as if all this was not real, and desperately trying to remain positive in a situation that had quickly spiralled out of our control.

On arrival at the Oxford hospital, we had to wait some time as they settled Matthew in to the Intensive Care Unit before we could go in and be with him. The wait did little to steady our nerves, nor prepare us for the shock of the paraphernalia that accompanied his care. There were wires and monitors everywhere. Lines into arteries, masks, machines, and that dramatic hiss and puff of the breathing apparatus as it artificially lifted and lowered our son's chest. With his eyes closed, he seemed so very far away from us as we stood there looking at him, tears falling unchecked down our faces. We wept together, for him, because of him, and to him. Our tightly clasped hands were now our joint prayer for him to be back with us, to complete our little family unit.

Later that day, still unconscious, Matt had a cerebral angiogram where a thin tube was inserted through a blood vessel in his groin and passed all the way up to his head, to inject dye into targeted arteries. This was to see if there was any blockage in his head causing the seizures and the abnormality on the CT scan and to ascertain whether Matthew had had a stroke.

Almost before we had time to fully digest the unbelievable possibility that our twelve year old son had suffered a stroke, we were informed that this was not the case. We didn't know how to react. Our emotions were rising and falling on some clinical rollercoaster. We were relieved that this particular diagnosis was not confirmed, but were immediately thrown into a different arena of shock as the doctors informed us of the possibility of a brain tumour. The life-support machine continued to hiss and puff as it lifted and lowered Matthew's chest for him.

Sometimes, the resilience of the human body to hear and process shocking information and maintain a degree of sanity or normality, amazes me. We sat listening, as specialists painted gloomy pictures we had no desire to see. Our son, a brain tumour? How could that be? We loved him too much. We had always looked after him. He was our son, not someone else's. This was real life, not some soap opera! The doctors scheduled an MRI scan, which takes extremely detailed pictures of the brain in slices thus showing up any irregularities. The life-support machine continued its mechanical breathing for our precious son.

Over the next two days, where time seemed to blur into one long and painful intake of breath, attempts were made to decrease the sedatives being dripped into Matt's veins to allow him to regain consciousness in preparation for the MRI scan. The hope was that the fitting could be controlled by special anticonvulsants as he was encouraged to breath for himself. But each time he started to regain consciousness, we witnessed small twitching movements in his face which developed into full blown seizures and he had to be sedated again. It was agonising to watch, my heart felt like it was shattering into thousands of sharp fragments inside my chest. I couldn't think about anything except our son. I was desperate to see his beautiful blue eyes open and look at us. I began to loathe the sound of the breathing machine.

Chapter 4

In those timeless first days visitors came and went, leaving love, hope, prayers and food for us. We did not feel like eating anything, but dutifully obliged, aware that our bodies needed fuel to maintain strength. We were at Mattie's bedside all day everyday and often long into the night. The hospital had arranged for a small room to be at our disposal for us to take it in turns to grab a few undisturbed hours of sleep. But sleep does not come easily when you lie weeping alone in the dark, your heart breaking.

Finally, late on the Sunday evening, three long days after his admission to Intensive Care, Matthew woke up seizure free. He looked very glassy eyed and distant. His actions were slow and disjointed and his face looked bloated from the drugs and assisted breathing. But he was our baby, back with us, and we thanked God as tubes were removed from his nose and throat. I hungrily drank in every detail of my son's precious, conscious body.

Although the MRI scan had been planned for the next day, for reasons unexplained, it did not take place and Matt was transferred from Intensive Care to the children's neurosurgical ward. The transfer was upsetting, Matthew was disorientated and obviously insecure. As we walked alongside his bed, we saw he was crying silently. So did we.

The ward was busy and noisy after the clinical peace of the Intensive Care ward. Instead of the one-to-one nursing, Matthew was one of many young patients, some of whom were extremely ill. He was put into a tiny room on his own, but staff were continually monitoring him, testing vital signs, blood pressure and temperature. It was not a peaceful environment and Matt had little sleep. Mark and I took it in turns to sleep on a mattress on the floor at his bedside, reaching up to touch him in an attempt to reassure ourselves of reality, but with all our stabilising landmarks moved, we could be flying upside down for all we knew!

Miraculously, by the following Tuesday, May 1st, Mattie had managed to eat a minute amount of food and taken some fluids by mouth. Was this progress? We prayed it was. Though he did not complain, we could see the main artery line inserted into his neck was bothering him but it was required to remain until after the scan to administer a general anaesthetic. As a mother I felt violated on his behalf. Tears came easily. He was like a pincushion from all the blood samples taken and drugs administered. But never a tangible sign of complaint. Sometimes he would look imploringly at us with his huge, expressive blue eyes if something was too painful – but he never cried out. It is extremely hard to observe your child endure so much intrusive nursing, even if you believe it is for their good, without wanting to interfere big time.

Meetings with the neurosurgeon revealed his reluctance to perform any kind of biopsy on the lesion in Matt's head. Inside the brain the shadow was in an area of extremely high risk. Still unable to diagnose Matthew's illness, it was suggested that he might have tuberculosis as some of his symptoms were similar and the doctors wanted to treat him with powerful antibiotics to combat that. I recall feeing a slight ease of tension. If it was tuberculosis, it was treatable, Matt could be well, we could go home, this nightmare over. Unbelievably I heard myself praying that my son's illness was tuberculosis.

He was given a cocktail of antibiotics, so strong that his vein soon collapsed as he lay in agony in his bed, with only the tiniest whimper audible from him. The injection, by continual intravenous drip, had only run a small proportion of its course. We called the doctors and asked them to stop this torture and find another way to give him the drugs he needed. I had an overwhelming desire to scoop Matthew up in our arms and run away with him. With hindsight, I wish we had. The days and nights continued to blur into one long nightmare. They stopped the antibiotics and for a time no more was said about tuberculosis.

After another agonising wait for the MRI scan, it was finally performed that Wednesday and the following evening Matthew was transferred again, this time to the John Radcliffe hospital out of town. It was good in a way to leave the bustle of the neurosurgical ward for the peace and coolness of a small room in the adolescent ward. But it was also scary to leave the hospital environment and staff we knew for more uncharted territory. I do remember feeling optimistic though, as the move confirmed that Matt did not require imminent brain surgery. They still had copious tests to perform, but it seemed we had moved forward. With hindsight I definitely would have scooped Matthew up and run far, far away!

So it was, one life-changing week after Matt was admitted to hospital, we were called to a meeting with the neurological consultant and two nurses. Two friends from our church accompanied us for support. As we sat in the small impersonal side room, the atmosphere felt heavy even before the consultant spoke. Grim news always carries its own oppression. Matthew didn't have tuberculosis. But from the results of the MRI scan, the doctors believed our son had cancer. They understood it to be in his brain, with a tumour in the frontal lobe area. It was in the meninges that cover the brain and spinal cord and in his central nervous system. At this stage, a full diagnosis was not available, but it appeared very aggressive. They advised us to spend the weekend together as a family and tell our son what was wrong with him.

Chapter 5

Inside I was shouting, "Oh God! Please help me." I wanted to disappear into outer space and scream, where no one could hear me. Outside, I held Mark's hand, trembled slightly and felt one solitary tear make a pathway down my cheek. I was aware of Mark, and of arms holding me. I was surprised to hear my own voice, as if through a tunnel, saying, "We believe that only Almighty God can heal our son, whether that's by conventional methods, alternative treatments or a miracle, doesn't matter. We will continue to pray."

All four of us walked across the hall to Matt's room. We just stood by the bed, unwilling to speak of the frightening prognosis we had been given. Matthew was a sensitive boy, we wanted to be careful what we said to him, we did not want to terrify him, we knew that if he saw us hurting it would affect him badly. Some days later, the neurologist again suggested we share our deadly news with Mattie before too much time had passed. We decided not to. With hindsight it is one decision I am glad we made.

The doctors expected rapid growth of the tumour and so decided to greatly increase his anticonvulsants. Following a huge dose, Matt became extremely distressed. One of us stayed with him constantly, the other one kept a vigil of prayer and weeping in the lonely, impersonal bedroom provided. During the next three days, although we managed to get Matthew to swallow some fluids, neither his condition nor the prognosis improved.

After a painful lumbar puncture to extract sample cells

for testing, we were informed by the oncologist that the unnamed cells looked particularly bad and very malignant. All you want to hear from doctors is whatever ails your child is nothing serious and they can cure it, quickly and painlessly. I honestly felt like slapping them for delivering such appalling news even though it was not their fault.

The list of sedative drugs he was being given grew longer, yet his sleep grew less and less. We both knew he was suffering. He seemed so brave yet so small. I think I always knew the human body could endure alarming levels of pain and survive. I now know the human mind can sometimes absorb huge chunks of devastating news without slipping over the precipice into insanity.

Matthew's tiny room had become our private hell on earth. We kept our spirits up when we were with him, talking to him cheerfully about anything and everything. Listening to music, pretending to watch television, hugging and kissing each other, praying for his healing and trying to display a lightheartedness we did not feel inside. Only when we were at a safe distance from his room, would the floodgates open and we'd cry, desperately, silently. Inside the room, Mark and I spoke to each other with meaningful looks, unwilling to verbalise our terrible secret. Although up to that point Matt was able to speak, he seemed to do so less and less. The build-up of drugs was claiming his cognitive thoughts.

The following Tuesday, May 8th, we managed to bath him and wash his neglected hair, his crowning glory. That was the last time we held him upright. The last time we were able to hug him properly. The heat from the bath triggered seizures again, something we later learned can happen, and as they gathered momentum the drugs were increased until that evening Matthew was readmitted to the Paediatric Intensive Care Unit. His respiratory system was greatly suppressed through the drugs and he needed twenty-four hour observation. It felt so painful to be there again but we had no choice. Back in the tiny impersonal parents' room, Mark and I passed another night without sleep, just crying in each other's arms.

Next morning, we were informed that Matt's condition was deteriorating and his prognosis was worsening. I wondered how much worse it could get. Seemingly much. We both caved in. Friends arrived within thirty life-stopping minutes and we leaned on them heavily. Our baby was once again intubated, with tubes and machines everywhere. He was again unconscious. Our lives hung suspended again, like drops of water on a leaf pulled inevitably downwards by gravity.

The oncologist advised that chemotherapy was imperative within the next twenty-four hours, but that lack of a confirmed diagnosis made it extremely difficult to prescribe the exact package. They said time did not permit a biopsy, as it would take too long for results to be available. It sounded so impersonal, like Matthew was an experiment. I wanted to keep telling them that, but I'm sure they were doing the best they could.

Huge life-changing decisions, so little understanding, seemingly no choice. We gave permission for powerful cytotoxic drugs to be administered into our son's body while he lay helpless and unconscious on his bed. We cried out for God to help us and deliver us from our fears and guilt.

The first series of injections were given that night; the nurse who gave them was seriously gowned and gloved-up for protection. Over the next week, Matthew remained unconscious while the chemotherapy insidiously released its potentially lethal cocktail into his system. We prayed that, like some impeccable marksman, it would find and destroy its target.

Chapter 6

Waiting is an enforced occupation in hospitals. You have little choice. The medical profession work busily, treating their patients, but for the family the wheels turn painfully slowly. We sat, we watched, we prayed. Frequent visitors came and went and gave us overwhelming love and support. But at the end of the day, it was still the two of us, watching our son, praying for a miracle and waiting.

One prayer was answered as five days later Matthew, once again able to breathe unaided, was transferred to the children's cancer ward, Ward 4B. The very words 'cancer ward' sent shivers through our bodies. It felt as though, by being there, we were accepting the diagnosis, the prognosis, the inevitable. The word 'cancer' conjures up an unstoppable, sinister attack that will inevitably end in an untimely, painful death.

Particularly at that time, I don't think Mark and I allowed ourselves to focus on anything negative. Instead, we just saw our horizon as the next day. If we got there, it was a victory. The next meal became a significant oasis in an arid desert. We focused on our son through a microscope of emotions. Feeling like inmates on death row, we watched his every breath, every utterance, every movement, with rapt attention not knowing if we had tomorrow.

The following days and weeks in Ward 4B were a draining experience mentally, physically and emotionally. Apart from the horrendous reality of what our son was going through, we suddenly became aware of a plethora of children suffering from life-threatening illnesses. The oncology ward joined onto the children's cardiac ward and shared common facilities. They also shared a common tension that permeated everywhere.

Our outlook on the world changed in those protracted weeks. We saw a level of suffering we previously knew nothing about. We glimpsed a world where children silently suffer. Where parents are torn apart with fear and anxiety. Where families fragment in the fallout of rampant disease. Thin little figures, in various stages of hair loss, walked up and down the corridors of ward 4B, trailing metal apparatus resembling mobile coatstands that fed toxic chemotherapy drugs into their systems.

As well as carrying out what seemed like endless tests, the doctors were continually questioning us about Matt's medical history, his lifestyle and anything unusual we may have noticed about his physical condition prior to his admission to hospital. Small seemingly insignificant things, viewed through the lens of hindsight, began to piece together an alarming picture surrounding the previous six months of Matt's life. Mark and I then found ourselves trading-off anxiety for guilt.

Apparently an unusual amount of sleeping is a trade mark of cancer. Looking back, we realised that Matt had slept a lot, especially during the lead up to his illness manifesting. But to be fair to ourselves we had to admit that adolescents can and do sleep an inordinate amount of time, especially in the mornings. Matthew peacefully passed many a Saturday morning snoozing in his bed and it was no ride in the park getting him up for school!

As I said, our family history of illnesses was pretty unremarkable. Colliding with adolescence, Matthew was a friendly, sensitive guy with a great sense of humour, always playing jokes on his very gullible parents. He was caring about others, and not given much to complaining, unless it was to exclaim, "You're so unfair!" in reply to most of our suggestions about his room, his homework, his hair, his bedtime. You know the kind of thing – normal family life with a soon-to-be teenager.

However, with hindsight other incidents were disturbing and it was some time before reason and good counselling from friends made us admit that, as isolated incidents, it would have taken detective work on the scale of Hercule Poirot to make a watertight case for the condition that felled Matthew.

One morning before school and running out of time as always, Matt did tell me that he couldn't get his shoe on. I glanced simultaneously at him and at the clock. "Why not?" I asked him, panic rising at the possibility of disrupting our tight schedule. He stood before me, body held in that typically awkward teenage pose and economically explained that his foot "felt funny". We'd had recent discussions about his desire for a new, trendier pair of school shoes, and I had explained that he had to wear his present, perfectly-sized ones for a few months before we could justify buying more. That morning, I asked him to put his shoe on and suggested we talk about it in the car on the way to school. In the morning rush it slipped my mind and he never mentioned it again.

Several weeks before that, entertaining a friend for tea, Matt had again assumed the 'position', this time holding one arm down to look much longer than the other. "My arm's all funny. Look Mum," he said, in his usual, non-urgent way. I did look and smiled, as I thought he was trying to make me laugh with a comical pose, as he often did. He didn't mention it again, and went off to hang out with his mate.

During lunch preparation for ourselves and hungry visitors one Sunday, Matthew walked past the dining room dresser on his way to the table and in doing so knocked several glasses onto the floor, breaking them. He then knelt down on the floor and strangely proceeded to lay down, amidst the broken debris. We helped him up checking he was all right. He was quiet, but no alarm signals went off in our heads. Enquiring about him later, our lunch guest, an ex-nurse, suggested that he might have been suffering from a small dose of embarrassment. Matthew never mentioned that incident again and, tragically, neither did we.

Chapter 7

The February before Matt's illness, we had taken a special holiday with two other families to Florida. It was a fantastic time, a longed-for break and Matthew enjoyed it all the more because our friends' children provided him with the company and fun he loved. We basked in welcome sunshine and visited places of interest. He seemed perfectly normal and invested lots of time swimming, which was his favourite sport. Tall for his age, and well built, he was a strong swimmer and the day-of-a-lifetime was spent swimming with dolphins. It seemed very expensive at the time, but with hindsight I thank God that we helped him realise one of his greatest dreams.

During the night flight home, following a day in the sun and the pool, Matt left his seat and joined Mark and I further down the plane saying that he felt a bit dizzy. When questioned, his friend commented that he had not eaten or drunk anything during the flight and we assumed he was dehydrated. He stumbled slightly against Mark, who helped him into the seat next to me where he promptly put his head in my lap and peacefully slept the remaining hours of the journey, displaying no adverse symptoms after our arrival back home. Another isolated incident – another piece of the jigsaw pieced together too late.

Two months later, Mark's job took him to Bahrain for a couple of days and as an extra treat, Matt and I were fortunate to be able to accompany him. We passed the time by the pool, swimming, chatting and laughing until Mark, having completed each day's work, joined us for precious family time. I remember one evening Matthew mentioning he had water in his right ear that would not come out. In an attempt to remedy this we had him lying with his head on one side hanging over the hotel bed. It was only with hindsight that I recall how odd it was he should complain of water in his ear, as thinking back I realised he had uncharacteristically not swam underwater on that trip.

We have since learned that some of the telltale signs of brain cancers, and the tumours that form causing pressure, are pins and needles or numbness in hands and feet. Uncharacteristic lack of co-ordination is also a telltale sign. Dizziness can sometimes be a form of seizure, especially when followed by deep sleep, and should therefore be investigated. Odd sensations in the head or ears can indicate problems and of course headaches can be a signpost to something being amiss. Interestingly, Matthew never mentioned suffering from any headaches, until that unforgettable night in April.

It would be all too easy to blame ourselves for missing the little signs and symptoms that preceded the sudden onset of Matthew's illness and believe me we have travelled that road. Caring family and friends joke with us about the big stick lurking in our emotional cupboard waiting to burst forth and clobber us in our soul-searching moments. But the truth is, they were exactly that, isolated signs and symptoms and our son was not one to fuss, as I have said. At an age where his physical body was undergoing so many changes inside and out, he shyly chose not to draw close attention to himself and anything that may have caused him alarm or pain.

For common everyday reasons, we misinterpreted those signs. In possession of knowledge we now have, it breaks my heart because I feel that I failed to look after our darling son, that I failed him in his need. The truth is, we have to live our lives without hindsight and do the best we can. That is one reason we have written this book, in the hope that it may help to save other precious lives.

Following a visit from a representative of the charity CLIC, Cancer & Leukaemia in Childhood, Mark and I were offered the use of a nearby house, provided for families in these situations whose children were incarcerated in hospital for protracted periods or whilst undergoing chemotherapy. It was somewhere we could put our carrier bags now bulging with belongings, and take it in turns to bath and rest, away from the constant bustle and pressure of the oncology ward. By any standards it was truly a haven of respite and we are so grateful for this charity's provision and compassion. But we found it almost impossible to switch off our seesawing emotions and relax as we were constantly aware of Matt and each other during those paradoxically short nights with long silent spaces to think.

Sometimes Matthew had moments of real lucidity. He spoke a little, smiled his old smile and seemed relaxed. We have always been a family to openly express our love, both verbally and by touch. I was forever saying, "I love you Mattie," all the more when he was silently enduring painful blood tests. One day, with blue eyes glazed and a ghostly pale complexion, he laboured to remove his oxygen mask and slowly and silently mouthed in reply, "Love you too." Then his arm dropped exhausted onto the bed. I think I was the only person who witnessed what he had done and I wept silently. I could not have stopped the tears if I had wanted to. Reality seemed light years in the past. He has not been able to declare his love in that way since then.

Unfortunately these moments were too often interspersed with signs of extreme anxiety, seizures and drug-induced symptoms. He became more withdrawn as time went on. It is difficult to know whether that was as a result of physical inability, pain, or fear. We made sure that one of us was always with him; it was the only continuity we could provide.

We became aware that his inability to speak, and the many stressful situations he endured, were conducive to bringing on seizures. Observing him constantly it slowly became apparent to Mark and I that the seizures were Matt's pressure valve. As well as any pressure that the tumour might be causing in his head, when things got too much, too painful to bear, he would suffer a fit. Sometimes it would be fleeting, other times it would seem endless. Each attack would be treated with increasing amounts of sedatives. Each attack would carry its own threat of a possible return to Intensive Care. We continued to walk the tightrope of fear.

Chapter 8

Soon after the chemotherapy Matthew's immune system began to suffer and show signs of the effects caused by such high levels of toxicity. He was given blood, platelet and magnesium transfusions, copious blood tests and suffered further painful lumbar punctures as the doctors tried to extract enough spinal fluid to gain an informative reading on the malignant cells. The days dragged on but we were no nearer a positive diagnosis. Intimidating-sounding cancers were ruled out. Lymphoma and leukaemia were crossed off the list. We held our breath and prayed.

Matt's eyes were tested for any sign of melanoma – a skin cancer that will often manifest in the eyes if it has spread to the brain. No sign, thank God! Daring to believe, we prayed on. Matthew was heavily drugged, yet frequently restless and unable to sleep. Another MRI scan was scheduled, to compare pre-and-post chemotherapy. In the meantime, Matt was changing physically before our eyes. Due to the urgency with which the chemotherapy was administered, we had been unable to crop his hair. Now, each time we touched or combed his crowning glory, great clumps fell mockingly onto his pillow. Chemotherapy does not just target malignant cells, but rapidly dividing healthy ones suffer as well.

Still the word 'melanoma' hung menacingly over everything. We found ourselves pouring over his skin like adult monkeys, closely examining every millimetre of his epidermis, looking for anything that may indicate melanoma. They continued tests on the cells they found and sent samples to other laboratories around the country for identification. Devastatingly, on the 31st May, the oncologist advised us that comparisons between MRI scans confirmed that the chemotherapy had not altered the tumour size. It was time to consider another option but, to be honest, we didn't much like the sound of it.

Apparently another tiny 'shadow' had shown up on the second scan, this time in the centre of the brain, where the spinal fluid is produced. Radiotherapy was the next possible step, but reluctant to delay for an appointment in the fully-booked Oxford hospital, the doctors arranged that Matthew would have a biopsy in four days' time and then transfer the following day to the Middlesex Hospital in London for preparation and treatment.

As I said, our knowledge of all things medical was limited, but I did remember that these same doctors were initially very reluctant to perform a biopsy because of the location of the tumour and the risks involved. Now, it was being recommended. All of it, the biopsy, the preparation, the radiotherapy, sounded horrendous. We toppled back over the cliff and hung on by our fingernails. I don't think I stopped sobbing for a couple of hours. Mark and I consulted a cross-section of people, including doctors, to try to decide what would be best for our son. It was very scary. We knew nothing about anything really, and we realised most people we consulted didn't know much either, including the doctors. What we heard were opinions and conjecture. What was at stake was our son's life.

What followed seemed like a setback to Matthew's treatment plans, but in retrospect perhaps it was meant to give us more time to think things through. As I said, some questions will have to remain unanswered this side of heaven, but Mark and I both adamantly agree that if we had known then what we know now, we would definitely have scooped Matthew up and headed home, seeking second opinions and other options before giving permission for the biopsy. We reluctantly assented on Friday 1st June but that night Matthew started a raging fever. The actual cause was never established, but it lasted all over the weekend in spite of antibiotics and the biopsy was postponed.

Matthew was still being subjected to copious blood tests and as lines were inserted everywhere it became increasingly difficult to locate his veins. After one particularly painful attempt to take blood, Matthew became really distressed, which upset us so much that we willingly agreed to the proposal that he be fitted with a Hickman Line. This is a device usually inserted for prolonged chemotherapy treatment, as it allows toxic substances to be rapidly dispersed into the bloodstream near the heart.

During this normally straightforward procedure under general anaesthetic, Mark and I, feeling like fish out of water, ventured out of our concrete and glass prison for some fresh air while Matt was in theatre. We eagerly arrived back well within the operation's estimated hour and a half, expecting to go immediately to the recovery room and see our son.

We stood in the aching gap left in the ward where his bed had stood, gripping each others' hand, pretending to look out of the window and remain calm. We couldn't, and our fears mounted as the ever-present nursing staff also began to show concern that their special patient wasn't back. Finally, after four nail-biting hours, we thankfully received word that we could accompany him back to the ward. We later learned that there had been serious complications as the line went into the wrong place, but, thank God, the surgeon had managed to correct it and complete the procedure successfully.

Looking back, it still feels as if we were starring in a medical drama where the scriptwriters had tried to include as many cliff hanging scenes as they could in the shortest possible time. We were left wondering what on earth had happened to our normal family life in so little time. We had been in hospital for five weeks, though it felt as if we had lived through several lifetimes.

People continued to visit, pray and support us in all manner of ways. During those fraught weeks it was only by the grace of God and the generosity of family, friends and strangers alike that we had enough finances to pay our bills and had no need to think about anything other than the welfare of our son. Our doctor had certificated Mark to be off work, due to the seriousness of our situation, but his job as a steward with an airline meant a meagre basic salary if he did not operate on trips.

Chapter 9

We spent the next agonising few days waiting for Matt to recover from the effects of the anaesthetic. The antibiotics gave him loose bowels, and he was anxious, rigid and jerking a lot. At least he wasn't subjected to prodding and poking around for blood samples anymore but he seemed very quiet and sad. I remember thinking how small he looked in the hospital bed even though his body was getting longer.

When doctors, consultants and surgeons meet with you to talk about illnesses, diagnoses, treatments and prognoses, there is often confusion in the information pipeline. I don't know why it feels like that but we certainly found it to be the case during our time in hospital with Matthew. When the surgeon came to speak to us and obtain our written permission for the biopsy, Mark and I distinctly got the impression that it would only involve a modest cut into Matt's skull to remove a small sample of cell tissue from inside his brain for testing. In our ignorance we envisaged a kind of microsurgery. We both understood depth when it came to the operation, but neither of us had comprehended anything to do with height or width.

An ambulance was booked for the next Sunday evening to transfer him back to the Radcliffe Infirmary for the biopsy the following day. I don't think any of us got any sleep that night. Matthew's surgery, though scheduled for the morning was tormentingly delayed until mid-afternoon, as an emergency case was dealt with. Mark held

31

his hand as he was initially anaesthetised, then, entrusting our son to the surgeon and to ease our nerves which felt like catgut stretched across a violin, we headed out of the hospital for some fresh air. Without previous discussion we found ourselves headed towards the nearest bookshop and once there, purposefully to the health section.

Several months previously, I had been concerned about a small lump on my back. It was itching all the time and seemed to be growing larger, changing shape and occasionally bleeding. I had made an appointment to see my local doctor but was unable to attend as by then we were otherwise engaged in Oxford. By chance I found myself talking to a lady in a supermarket about a fortnight before Matt became ill. We got onto the subject of health and she mentioned that her adult daughter had died from melanoma the previous year. Until dissuaded by medical doctors, she had been using alternative treatments alongside the conventional ones and showed promising signs of improvement. The lady was convinced that the alternative treatment was working and discontinuing may have contributed to the relapse that preceded her daughter's death. I filed the information somewhere in the recesses of my mind and thought no more about it until our sojourn in Oxford. We picked up several books on diet and alternative treatments and headed back in time to collect Matthew from the recovery room.

On our way, we saw the operating surgeon on his ward round and asked how the procedure had gone. He said it passed without incident and reassured us they would be able to diagnose the cancer very soon. We went to see Matt, feeling slightly more positive for the first time in weeks. Our optimism was, however, short lived. As we walked towards his bed in the recovery room, it felt as if the floor was being pulled out from under our feet again.

A menacing bright red gash in his head, held together by ugly metal staples, ran from his crown and stopped just short of his right ear. His remaining sparse hair was matted with blood and his swollen head looked grossly lopsided. An involuntary shocked gasp escaped Mark's throat before he checked himself and smiled hesitantly. My stomach lurched and the area around my coccyx tingled with fear. Feeling that my legs would buckle, I managed to gently stroke Matthew's cheek and as his eyes slowly flickered open, I smiled and said, "Hello my darling boy, I love you!" Mark's face was pale and drawn, I'm sure mine was too. We silently pushed our fearful emotions way down inside and spoke soft reassuring words as we accompanied Matt back to his room.

He was given painkillers that evening as Mark went to the CLIC House to rest and I settled down to keep watch over him. I must have fallen asleep until sometime after midnight when I was aware of Mattie making small moaning noises. My heart almost stopped as I examined him. His head on the right-hand side was swollen almost to double its size. He felt burning hot and was obviously distressed and in pain. He was noticeably paralysed down his left-hand side and unable to speak.

I called the nurse who alerted the doctor on call and, after being examined, Matt was hurriedly taken for a CT scan. I called Mark and, by the time he arrived, we were informed that Matthew had a blood clot deep in his brain as a result of the operation and the next twelve hours were critical. The blood clot needed to disperse but they did not want to reopen his brain, as it may have aggravated the situation.

Here we were, slipping over into the abyss again into even darker, unplumbed depths. Over and over again for the remainder of that night, we cried out to the God we trusted to deliver our son from this nightmare.

Chapter 10

Our prayers were answered and Matthew survived the night, though his head was still very swollen and he was feverish. It was a good sign apparently, though at that stage we were so emotionally numb we seemed incapable of registering any signs as good. When the surgeon appeared on his ward round, accompanied by numerous colleagues and student doctors, I quietly asked how big the tumour was, how it looked, and if they knew anymore. Matt was conscious, though looking more like a punch bag than our beautiful son.

The reply seemed to scythe my husband from behind, his legs almost collapsed underneath him as the surgeon coldly stated, "Oh the whole brain's abnormal, all brown and granulated!" I took Matt's hand in mine and said for everyone's benefit, "Well, we could certainly do with some good news around here couldn't we Mattie?" The oppressive atmosphere remained heavily in the room for some time after they left.

I had always wondered how parents with very sick children coped with seeing them every day, looking little like their precious child and more like some poignant fund-raising advert. Illnesses like cancer can be cruel on appearances, and conventional treatment, which you may grasp with eager parental hands, seems often as cruel as the underlying condition.

In the six weeks Matthew had been in hospital his appearance had altered almost beyond recognition.

Following the course of chemotherapy, gone was his beautiful healthy hair – albeit which he latterly chose to wear long, lank and gelled over his face – and now his body suggested the ravages of war rather than treatment intended for his good. My tears flowed unchecked as I cut off the last of his hair, and even that could not be achieved with the dignity of a proper hair cut, as I had to just lop off what and where I could. I silently asked him to forgive us.

Of course, I have now come to understand that when all is said and done, your child is still your child and it doesn't matter what they may look like outside because, as parents, you only see the child that is within – and you just love them. You hurt with them when they hurt, you want to make everything all right for them, but you can't and so you go through everything with them because they mean everything to you. For me, that's a miniscule glimpse of how God sees us, His children. It doesn't matter what we look like on the outside, He loves us with or without hair, warts and all.

The consultants seemed in a rush to move on to the next stage of Matthew's treatment and whilst we understood their reasoning, because they were unsure of how much time we had, Mark and I were more keen to see Matt given time to recover from the onslaught of the operations, anaesthetics and drugs he had already endured before embarking on a ruthless course of radiotherapy. It is generally accepted that, paradoxically, the fitter you are before undergoing radiotherapy the better.

Obviously, you cannot be perfectly well because there would be no need for the treatment, but ideally not fresh from the operating table! "Years ago," I wrote in a letter to friends, "it used to be that people were expected to remain in hospital for a couple of weeks post-operation and facilities were then provided for them to go somewhere convivial for good old convalescence. It's all very well when people boast of their speedy return to normal everyday life and work after serious surgery, but our bodies need time to recover from illnesses and treatments, even in this fast-paced 21st century!"

It was intended that Matt should leave for London the morning after his biopsy, but even to our untrained eyes his condition screamed out for more care and rest. So with a new-found inner strength, we insisted he stay put until we felt he was well enough to continue further treatment. After another transfer back to ward 4B in the other hospital the Paediatric Registrar there wholeheartedly agreed with us and so we gained some precious time for Matthew. He looked the most poorly I had ever seen him, every inch a very sick cancer patient. How could our son have changed so drastically in such a short space of time?

Chapter 11

Over the next few days we stayed with Matt constantly, only briefly leaving his room to take a shower or change clothes. During that time, with the encouraging assistance of the wonderful oncology nurses, we undertook more and more of Matthew's daily routine care. Because he was eating very little before the biopsy, he had to be fed with liquid food through a naso-gastric tube. That is a thin plastic tube, uncomfortably inserted into one nostril and passed down the throat to the stomach, where it delivers sustenance directly into the patient's body.

This was now his only means of being fed, as the post-biopsy paralysis had adversely affected his swallowing. He had a catheter fitted and his incontinence now meant that he could do nothing for himself. Mark and I kissed him gently, loved him passionately and took all our frustrations out on each other, as silently as possible. We are by nature very hopeful, optimistic people, but we were both haemorrhaging emotionally and spiritually and the outlook seemed grim.

We spent all our time at Matt's bedside holding his hand, talking to him, encouraging him and reading everything we could find connected with cancer, treatments, diet and alternative therapies. Friends researched the internet for us – and even brought a computer to the hospital for us to make contact with the outside world ourselves. But, most of all, we read our Bibles and prayed – to a God we knew, a God we trusted, a

God who loved us and who had promised never to leave us, even if it didn't feel quite like that!

Painfully slowly, Matthew's vital signs began to show minute signs of improvement, but still no results were forthcoming from the biopsy sample. The only information that filtered through was that someone thought the malignant cell markers resembled melanoma and more tests were being carried out. The following Monday morning, exactly a week since the biopsy, we saw the consultant who made the decision to continue with the original plan anyway and transfer Matt to London. As he left the room to book the ambulance, Mark and I felt our grasp on the situation, along with our hope, draining away.

Then, suddenly, we were summoned to see the consultant in his office. We nervously approached the door and entered. He invited us to sit down. I think we sat. Then he told us that he had just received a call from the laboratory confirming that the cells were melanoma cells. He said that Matthew had a primary malignant melanoma in the frontal lobe area of his brain and the malignant cells were present all over the lining of his brain and in his spine and therefore affecting his entire central nervous system.

There was nothing more they could do for Matthew and he mentioned a life expectancy of eight to twelve weeks. The options were to have Matt admitted to a hospice for care or, if we preferred, we could take him home and care for him ourselves. Down a long, muffled tunnel I heard him asking Mark if he had understood what had been said or if he needed it explaining again as he didn't seem cognisant. Mark smiled and my hearing became clear as he said, "I'm sorry, I understand everything you have just said, but I don't believe that is what's going to happen to our son."

Neither of us relinquished our hold on the other's hand.

We exchanged silent purposeful looks and I said, "Home, we want to take Mattie home." We left the consultant's office with our heads miraculously upright and clung to each other all the long walk back the 'green mile' to the ward and Matthew's room. Smiling as we entered, hardly able to contain our joy, eyes filling with tears of relief, we kissed him and kissed him, then hugged the nurse and said in unison, "We're going home Mattie, we're going home."

Mark writes:

In all the time the Matt was in hospital, from the moment we called the ambulance to the time we took him home, I can honestly say my faith in God never wavered. But it wasn't always that way. When I was twenty-four my dad died prematurely a few weeks after being badly injured in a car crash while working in Africa. I begged God not to let him die but, from my perspective, He did. I decided I didn't want anything else to do with a God like that. But through an amazing sequence of events, I became what some would call a 'born again' Christian in the mid 1990's and committed my life to Jesus. Since then, there have been times of heartache and trials, though nothing compared to Matt's illness, and yet, through it all, I know it is only my faith that has enabled me to keep living when I felt so broken and defeated.

Much of the technical jargon that we heard in hospital didn't make sense; all I knew was my main man was gravely sick but I trusted God with his life and mine. Lynette is a far more outwardly emotional person than me. You always know what she's thinking because she verbalises it. I turn inwards, inside myself. I think that's how God has been able to strengthen me, because He's in there, inside me with my pain in the place I don't allow anyone to go.

Chapter 12

Matthew's birth, a couple of months after my fortieth birthday, was the culmination of the great relationship Mark and I enjoyed. Our life together was by no means idyllic; we didn't live on a cloud of love, joy, peace and patience, but we really relished each other's company, spent a great deal of time together and had an extremely good friendship undergirding our love.

More than a little aware that my body clock was ticking away, and immediately following a miscarriage, we eagerly awaited the addition to our little unit. To say we were besotted with our precious baby boy is an understatement. He was 'simply the best' as the song goes. To us he was perfect in every way from the second we laid eyes on him and our feelings never altered. Although like most new parents we had names in mind for our child, nothing seemed suitable until we settled on Matthew, just before we took him home to live with us. It means 'gift from God'.

I vividly remember carrying my treasured bundle in my arms around the maternity ward of the hospital looking at all the other new mums and their charges. It struck me how the other newborns didn't seem nearly so beautiful compared to my son – even the girls! Motherhood for me was a wonderful thing, it came complete with a very large pair of rose coloured glasses and it did seem then that life for us was rosy. During my maternity leave we had enough money to pay our bills and unlike many women with babies, I enjoyed the security of a loving and supportive partner. I returned only to part-time work after a protracted maternity leave and Mark and I juggled our shifts so that one of us was nearly always with Matt.

Growing up, Matthew was an energetic child to be with. From early on he displayed a zest for life that urged him to try anything and do everything and he approached most things with that childlike innocence that says, "I am, therefore I can!" Coupled with that, he was a very affectionate boy and as he developed it became more and more apparent that he had a tenderness and compassion for others far beyond his years.

Within a few months of Matt's birth, I discovered I was prematurely menopausal. It was a huge shock and momentarily left me gasping on the scrapheap of life, but Matt's happy disposition and adventurous personality kept me extremely busy in my new role as mum and gave so much pleasure that I resigned myself to no further children and, with Mark, basked in the joy of our only son.

Early knowledge of Matthew's status as an only child made us considerably aware of his pressing need for friends and companionship. So even before he was able to speak, our house was usually bursting at the seams with 'little Lilliputians'. Mark earned the nickname of the Pied Piper because, wherever he went, he was always accompanied by Matt and his mates. Whenever we arranged outings, the first question we were confronted with was, "Who's coming with us?" Friendships were supremely important to Matthew. His first and dearest friend he knew almost from birth, and all his other relationships were of long standing with mates he saw frequently and loved dearly. It is an accolade to our son that they felt the same about him.

School was a good and not-so-good experience for Matt. It was extremely good because he was able to be with his friends all day, but not so good because the education authority had another agenda, learning! Like all children Matthew was a unique individual, fortunately quick to learn and particularly artistic. He had favourite and much less favourite subjects but mostly attempted all things. He had fairly high self-imposed standards and would often be discouraged if he did not meet them. In his early years we were just happy for him to be happy. There was time enough, we concluded, for serious application to studies. We both wanted Matt to enjoy his experiences of life and develop emotionally and spiritually. Academics would maybe come later!

Ever etched in my memory is one incident that grows funnier with passing years but at the time caused me to badly fail the test of level-headed parental understanding and forgiveness. It's odd how our priorities change with passing years. It was the morning after a sleepover at our house and, following what can only be described as exemplary behaviour by Matt and his chum Simon, the deadline for returning surplus children was extended in a rush of loving expression on my part. With hindsight, I would always maintain that such schedules are strictly adhered to. Extensions are known to invite the inevitable hiccoughs!

Investigating a prolonged time of quiet, I ventured upstairs to see how the lovely lads were doing. They were doing just fine! They had transformed the decor in our bedroom long before it was ever fashionable for interior designers to indulge in 'changing rooms'. Armed only with bright red and orange felt tip pens and with deft precision they had added their personal touches to numerous surfaces, including, but not limited to, an antique white bedcover, a newly-upholstered pale yellow armchair, lampshades, walls and, as I was later to discover, the walls and tiles in our newly-decorated bathroom. All executed with an avant-garde flair to be admired, but unfortunately not by me and not then.

It is a miracle of nature that my jaw did not require resetting as I gasped, gaped and yes, cried, at the scene before my eyes. Each individual attempt at decoration resembled the mark of Zorro. What baffled me was how two fairly small children had been able to make contact with the lampshade suspended from a high ceiling with the accuracy of trained marksmen. Trampolining on the bed of course! 'That incident', as it is still referred to by us and Simon's mum, did little for my reputation as a rational mother, but, as I said, the passing years have been kinder to the memory than I was that day to the un-caped crusaders.

Chapter 13

We soon realised our extremely sociable child's main daily objective was to be in the company of those he counted as friends. When he was, his ability and achievement flowed out of that contentment and we had a very happy live wire on our hands. Out of necessity, our kitchen table has always been large to accommodate friends at tea time. The atmosphere in our small Victorian town house was inevitably one of activity and noise. It was a special place to be. Indoor dens, the magical dressing-up box, marbles, cars, swords and popular collectibles littered rooms and children, including Mark, littered every nook and cranny during the inevitable game of 'hide and seek'. Halcyon days indeed!

One aspect of my relationship with Mark has always been a strong sense of humour and an ability to laugh with each other, eventually, in most situations. Matthew most definitely inherited that invaluable quality. We were always exposed to his wacky view of life and were willing victims of his jokes. Ever the gentleman, though, he would always encourage his incorrigible dad, whilst commiserating with me at the umpteenth hearing of Mark's repertoire of jokes.

The number of children you may have, as well as being biological, is also a very personal decision. There are pros and cons for one or more. For us, though, our little unit had expanded to three and we liked it. Even beyond the natural season of a young child's total dependance upon its parents, we remained exceptionally close and did almost everything together. We were the Three Musketeers – all for one and one for all. In all the time Matt was growing up Mark and I were only parted overnight from him during one brief sojourn with school and sleepovers at nearby friends' houses. It was our choice. It was what we wanted more than anything.

During Matthew's childhood we lived within walking distance of the town of Windsor in England. It was a favourable place to grow up, boasting its own castle and rich history. Schools were of a good standard and, during our time there, operated a three tier system, meaning that children attended their first school until the age of eight, then went to a middle school until they were thirteen before moving to senior school to concentrate on all the official exams. Whether one system works more efficiently than another is a complex question that I won't address here.

With hindsight, I don't think the change to a large middle school at the tender age of eight was personally right for Matthew. He found the transition from his small infant school to a huge establishment quite daunting and experienced a difficult and stressful first year there before he began to adjust. Where once he and his friends were all in the same class, they were now scattered amongst many classes. One main form teacher teaching most subjects was replaced with many specialist teachers, and his familiar world that centred around one classroom all day dramatically changed as he had to navigate his way around noisy school corridors amongst a hugely differing age and behavioural range of children.

We noticed a change in Matt about this time. His quirky humour would still surface at home but he seemed different, somehow quieter and burdened down with school work. Whilst he doted on his friends, he was quite shy in crowds and unsure of himself. His stature meant he wasn't bullied at school and, although apparently well-liked by his peers, he was slow to establish relationships outside the circle of friends he already knew. He had developed a strong sense of justice and his loyalty to his mates often found him in the firing line from teachers.

Not being one to complain, I think he internalised a lot of the day-to-day stuff that school children have to deal with and it took a long time for us to establish that he felt very lonely at this time in his life, even and especially amidst six hundred other pupils.

One activity we have always made time for as a family is holidays. Working in the travel industry has meant that we were privileged to be able to do this perhaps more than most but, even when we had little surplus funds, we would always try to find some way to get away together. Tents of the leaking canvas and trailer variety, ageing caravans and plusher camper vans have all been tested and found enormous fun by our family and any extra companions we could cram in. Matt loved travelling from an early age, especially to other countries, though he didn't always grasp the fact that we were often on standby tickets and consequently could not plan too far ahead, nor guarantee our departure date or, indeed, choice of destination.

We were fortunate enough to visit the wonderful world of Disney on more than one occasion, accompanied, of course by the compulsory companions. The make-believe, fun and plastic perfection of those holidays was something that captured all our imaginations, not just Matt's. As I mentioned earlier we were especially blessed during one such vacation, shortly before his illness became apparent, to spend time swimming with dolphins and fulfilling a precious dream for our intrepid traveller and we have the inevitable pictures of us all kissing a dolphin to prove it!

Cars were an avid hobby of Matthew's. Drawing them,

riding in them, identifying them and generally enjoying them. It's fair to say that he was encouraged in this pastime by his father, who just loves cars, any cars, new, old, functioning or lost causes. Mark had earned himself the nickname as the Robin Hood of the car trade, long before we ever met, due to his unique ability to buy old heaps, usually from people richer than us, spend time and money getting them roadworthy and selling them on to those he considered poorer than us at greatly reduced prices! Mark and Matt would often disappear for many hours down to the car auctions, just looking of course. And all in the days before mobile phones could track down my inmates who had gone absent without official leave!

It's probably just as well that Matt was clued-up where cars were concerned, as our family always seemed to be trying out yet another second-hand model and it was often only his acute powers of observation that enabled me to identify which one we were using at any particular time we left the house.

Growing up, perhaps one of Matt's greatest gifts was that of mimicry. Accents were his speciality and he had a seemingly inexhaustible repertoire of cartoon characters. In typical childlike fashion he would watch films, especially cartoons, many times over and his retentive mind would commit to memory whole episodes with which he entertained us every day. His ability to recreate whole scenes was heightened by his keen observation of small details and great facial expressions. Mark and I didn't fare too badly either. With the daily bathtime routine incorporating 'live' shows for Matt with our hands stuffed up countless glove puppets, we too acquired a pretty extensive repertoire. Sooty, Sweep, Cousin Scampy, and Ed the Duck still bear the scars from treading the boards nightly.

It wasn't always the obvious that attracted Matthew. He

loved humour that was capable of laughing at itself in a subtle off beat way. A born animal lover, his combined tastes found him enjoying Garfield, Bugs Bunny, Deputy Dawg, Donald Duck, Road Runner, Wallace & Gromit and many other colourful characters alongside blockbuster movies that immortalised toys and their zany approach to life.

Two of his heroes, and my all-time favourites, would have to be Woody and Buzz Lightyear from 'Toy Story'. Although quickly able to imitate most of the characters in that first film, it was these two mates that captured his imagination. Matt was my own personal little Buzz Lightyear, always looking out for me when Mark was away working. We would walk to school re-enacting his favourite scenes, saving the universe and other day-to-day stuff. My son never failed to brighten my day.

Little things that you say and do can come to mean so much. I would always say, "I love you, Mattie," and he would always reply, "Love you too, Mum," except outside the school gates of course! Sometimes we'd embark on a seemingly silly exercise of declaring more love for each other by adding numerically to the statement. For example, "I love you 37!" Reply: "I love you 468!" and so on, continuing as long as our capacity for mental arithmetic allowed and ending with the penultimate declaration to be, "Love you infinity," and then Matt would always finish with "Love you infinity and beyond!" And we'd exchange looks verifying that statement.

It's funny how that particular habit never altered even after he outgrew the toys he so treasured. They joined an ever-growing band of old friends hanging out on his bed but we perpetuated their dialogue continuing to incorporate it into our everyday lives. Precious reminders of growing up. Now, as we prepared to take our son home for his biggest challenge, we couldn't help wondering whether with hindsight we could possibly have squeezed another drop of joy from the pages of his short life.

Mark writes:

When Lynn was pregnant, I can remember being incredibly excited. I wanted a son so very much at that time. It never entered my head that we might have a daughter; I don't know why because girls are great too, but then I was particularly ready for a son. To play with, teach, talk to, wrestle with, kiss, hug – all the things parents want to do with their children. I was ecstatic when Matt was born. Of course, to me, he was the most beautiful baby in the world. I was overwhelmed with the privilege of watching his birth. When it came to phoning people to tell them the news, I dialled their numbers but I couldn't speak because I was crying so many tears of joy.

But now I have sat by my son's bedside and cried tears of desperation. He was on powerful anticonvulsant drugs and none of the side effects were what you would wish your child to have. Some caused him to hallucinate, thinking he was on a high building, going to fall off. He would hold onto us so tightly. And he kept imagining he could see people and things in his room. It was all very scary stuff which reduced me to tears as I wrestled with him just to keep him on the bed. Since Matt's birth, I have kissed him, hugged him, played with him, prayed with him – and the joy of that is indescribable. But the pain of stroking him, kissing him and smelling his skin when he is unconscious after fitting, or from drugs enough to knock four guys out, has broken my heart.

Matthew endured two periods in intensive care, been ventilated and unconscious from drugs and examined by countless doctors, nurses and specialists. On each change of shift he would see a new one and each in turn would ask him the same countless questions about how he felt. He nearly always managed to reply politely "Fine." He was so brave. He didn't complain or shout about anything, although we often saw anxiety in his eyes and we know many of the tests carried out were not pleasant. It was hard enough for Lynette and I to get our heads around what was happening, but we couldn't imagine what Matt was feeling. I am sure he was in shock from the trauma. I was on my knees every day for him to feel safe and be at peace.

He had difficulty speaking and so couldn't express himself very well verbally, but in rare glimpses of the old Matt, he would say something funny or make a great face and even managed to pucker up and offer a kiss to a nurse. He knew he was very poorly and that the doctors were trying to help him get better, and I am sure he was aware when his hair fell out due to the chemotherapy that he had cancer. But the way he coped was an incredible example to me and I was determined to hang in there, to be there for him, no matter what happened.

Chapter 14

So it was, on 21st June 2001, two months after leaving hurriedly in the middle of the night, that we brought our beloved son back home. It had been our heart's cry for many weeks and we had promised him we would not leave the hospital without him. God does answer prayers. The countless arrangements that had to be made for it to be possible was no small thing. Matthew had to have a special bed, similar to the one he had in hospital, as he was hardly able to move and pressure sores were an ever-present threat. Miraculously, a super new one was delivered to the house in preparation for our homecoming. It was state-of-the art, all moving, singing and dancing – up, down, half up, half down – wonderful!

Mark and I were expertly trained in all aspects of caring for Matthew. Whilst we had greatly participated in the hospital it is another thing entirely to nurse someone requiring twenty-four hour care at home without constant back-up on hand. The nurses and doctors were wonderful in helping us achieve an acceptable level of capability in so short a time. The organisation for the medication alone was mind-blowing. We had to learn how to administer his medicines, including sedatives for seizures, how to operate the suction machine for his throat and the apparatus that pumped food into his body. All the nurses who had played a part in Matt's specialised care for the past two months had done so with that wonderful gifting that allows them to truly reach out in love to their patients; they were professionals all, but more than that, they were fellow humans who truly cared for us. We felt incredibly nervous, and inadequate but that was coupled with feelings of enthusiasm that we could actually do this for Matt. It seemed perfectly natural somehow and an extension of the love we felt for him.

Finally, it was all arranged – and in record time apparently. With such a poor prognosis, Mark and I had it clearly spelled out to us what we should expect over the next two months or so. It was a depressing picture of Matthew's expected deteriorating condition. That he would suffer more and more seizures as the pressure in his brain increased; that he would be conscious less and less, until eventually his body would be unable to survive his degenerative illness and he would die, probably in less than three months. We listened to everything that was said but headed homeward that day nonetheless feeling free, hopeful and expectant.

We opted for an ordinary ambulance home, as one with a paramedic crew may have delayed our departure and we were eager to get going. Mark accompanied Matthew and a nurse in the ambulance and I drove our car. Leaving home under emergency conditions had meant we were ill-prepared for a prolonged stopover and, as I set off towards home with a few supermarket bags of our belongings, it seemed a rather poignant visual statement of the unexpected turn our lives had taken. When your child is diagnosed with a terminal illness, material possessions and comforts take a back seat.

The June sunshine made the return journey extremely hot but the ambulance, making good time, arrived at the house soon after me and despite the doctors' fears, Matthew didn't suffer any seizures. If we ever needed confirmation that coming home was the best thing for

Mattie, we certainly had it as the ambulance crew wheeled him around through the back patio doors to the lounge and onto his bed. He gave the biggest smile we had seen for ages, albeit a one-sided one as he was still paralysed down his left-hand side.

Our house looked beautiful. I hardly recognised it – it was spotlessly clean and thanks to dear friends there were flowers everywhere. It was breathtaking! The sun was shining, the patio doors were wide open and a cool breeze was blowing through the whole house; it was perfect for our homecoming. The garden looked amazing, nothing like we remembered, but with countless pots and tubs spilling over with all kinds of blooms on the patio, creating an exciting panorama of colour and all visible from Matthew's bed that had been placed in the lounge.

It was very emotional coming home, but the presence of love already awaiting us there was tangible. Family welcomed us and settled us in, together with Sarah, our community nurse. The fridge and food cupboards were stocked with delightful goodies; it always amazes me how other people's shopping expeditions look far more exciting than mine.

Though tiring and a completely new learning curve for Mark and me, the first week at home was incredibly strengthening for us all. We felt very safe and secure in our home surroundings. We had back-up from our GP's surgery as well as the local community nurses. We promptly tested their ability to reach us quickly as Matt had been home less than twenty-four hours when he pulled his feeding tube out. He suffered a high temperature one night and what seemed like a possible infection, where a line had been previously inserted for blood samples in his wrist – but, despite all that, we both felt very buoyant in those early days.

Chapter 15

Based on everything we had recently learned, we promptly started Matthew on a healthy regime aiming to supply his body with vital nutritional requirements as soon as we could. Vitamins, minerals, amino acids and essential fats were among the daily supplementation we made to his liquid diet. When we first came home, he was being fed with a complete soya milk formula that was supposed to supply this healthy balance to his body. We had already changed from a dairy-based formula in the hospital after discovering it contained high levels of sugar and its derivatives, but were also disappointed to realise the soya formula replacing it was much the same. Our investigations revealed high levels of sugar consumed in any form were likely to feed tumours and suppress the immune system, seriously undermining its ability to combat illness.

I had read how beneficial food in pure juice form could be for our bodies, but it needed to be as fresh as possible, especially in sickness to deliver vital nutrients into the bloodstream within about thirty minutes. Through the internet we also learned how the preparation of fresh juices had a significant effect on the level of efficacy. There are lots of juicers on the market, but not all do the same job. We wanted one that provided optimum benefits. In the meantime, aware that fresh is best but for lack of any other option, we began giving Matt bottled organic juices whilst slowly reducing his milk formula.

With miraculous timing, dear friends raised some much-needed cash for us and we were able to purchase a juicer that met all our requirements within a couple of weeks of returning home. We spent any spare time we had reading, making phone calls and gathering as much information as we could about disease, its relationship to nutrition and alternative treatments for cancer. Had Matthew been able to speak, I'm sure he would have expressed surprise at his parents' skills. Our brush with technology had previously enabled us to send and receive e-mails, end of story. Now, we were 'surfing' with the best of them.

However, it was no easy thing to completely change Matt's feeding programme from the traditionally accepted formulas exclusively to freshly prepared juices. We had quite a battle on our hands when we explained our desire and reasons for stopping the milk feed. We were visited by a dietician from the hospital who asked us countless questions about the content of our proposed feeding regime.

The hardest task was convincing the medical representatives of the nutritional value of fresh juices, as opposed to just the calorific content, especially when administered to a diseased body. They seemed acutely aware of the calorific value of foods but we found their acceptance of the nutritional benefits of fresh juices to be slow. The calorific value of Matthew's diet seemed of far more importance to them than the dangerously high levels of sugar the processed feeds contained. We understood their concern to maintain adequate levels of vital vitamins and minerals in his body but it was not always easy to challenge an established mindset.

For example, we were shown a printed guideline used by the hospital dietician to assist young people to increase their potassium intake. The recommendations included chips, as potatoes contain high levels of potassium. We already knew that cooking depletes the benefits contained in many foods and the saturated fats chips are inevitably cooked in could cause more harm in the long term.

Matthew's continued need of a feeding tube limited how we administered his food to him and so we were acutely aware that the quantity provided needed to deliver maximum quality. It took a lot of discussion to persuade the medical representatives but Mark and I remained insistent and finally changed Matthew over to a liquid diet of fresh vegetable and fruit juices alongside supplements, all without any sugar, sweeteners, additives, dairy products or soya substitutes containing processed oils.

Initially everything was done under the surveillance of the dietician who was guided by the government's recommended daily allowance (RDA) guidelines. But our continued research highlighted the need for careful adjustments to those guidelines when dealing with the immune system of patients with serious illnesses. Because Matthew's nutritional needs were so unique, we soon found ourselves beyond the scope and direction of the hospital dietician and once again very much out on our own.

We also discovered it is not always easy or simple to receive assistance that may be available to care for someone at home. The local doctors and community nurses do all they can to assist, but they are part of an already overloaded national health system in the United Kingdom and have to rely to a greater degree on the carers to do as much as they can for their patients.

With no previous knowledge or experience to draw on, and with family and friends sacrificially rallying round to assist financially as much as they could at the outset, we were slow to realise and seek what assistance was available. Our ignorance delayed us making claims for allowances and in so doing we sometimes lost out, as certain social services payments will not be back-dated. Also, as we discovered to our cost, it can take hours to complete forms with the infinite details required for benefits, and it is advisable to get someone to make preliminary enquiries on your behalf as soon as you think you may need assistance.

As well as certain financial help, we discovered we were also entitled to practical items needed for Matt's care but we found that we often had to make persistent enquiries in order to receive all the necessities. Just to approach the organisations concerned was very time-consuming and, to be honest, we often found we had neither the energy or tenacity for such tasks. For example, we discovered that incontinence pads are allocated to patients by the health service without taking into account individual needs. As our son was a big lad it soon became apparent that the statutory daily allowance was never going to be sufficient. We hadn't anticipated we would have to aggressively seek special consideration from understanding individuals working in a restrictive system. These issues and ordering and collecting repeat medical prescriptions for Matthew, all took up valuable time and it was a huge bonus when others could assist in the process.

The days were long and tiring. Outside our windows the sun shone heralding summer but inside we lived out a strange season-less existence, like life in some far off galaxy. We spent most of our time in the lounge, making forages to the kitchen, bathroom and occasionally the front door to take collection of supplement consignments. Matthew's special air bed was operated electronically and although Mark and I eventually learned to sleep in spite of it, the noise was something we were always aware of. We discovered that even with a pillow under your head, you could still hear incessant hissing as air circulated through the mattress. Matt never made any sign of complaint though I knew he was aware of it. I once asked him if it was awful having to listen to it all day long. He answered gently though falteringly, "Yeees."

Mark and I couldn't go out without intricate pre-planning as Matthew's care required two people all the time. One person could not move him in the bed alone and because of his paralysis, we had to assist him in all his bodily functions. Offers of help were always available from family and friends and we took them up on their generosity from time to time, but because both of us had been caring for Matt for such a prolonged period of time, we knew the routines and worked well with each other. Also, as his parents, we both wanted to be with him as much as possible and neither of us felt comfortable away from his bedside for too long.

Fortunately our lounge was large and we were able to accommodate two guest beds in there as well as all the equipment for Matthew and other furniture. When Matt first came home, he hardly slept at night. As soon as it became dark he seemed fearful, staring ahead, seemingly at nothing. His two-month stay in hospital and all the operations had deeply affected him and there was little difference it seemed between day and night. It sometimes helps if you are in a small side room off the main hospital ward, but even there you cannot escape the continuous activity and the lights. Most nights, Matthew had to undergo frequent checks, including blood pressure and visual responses, which meant even if he had fallen asleep, uncomfortable machines were attached to his body or lights were shone in his eyes – all of which is standard procedure in hospital, but it took its toll on his sleeping cycle.

Reluctant to leave him awake on his own, we devised a shift pattern where one of us would sit awake for four hours by his bed while the other one would try to sleep at the opposite end of the room, as far away from the hissing bed as possible! When friends offered practical help at night, we would luxuriously divide the shifts into three and take it in turns to go upstairs for a precious four hours of hopefully undisturbed sleep. But we were continually tired and as a result small issues could quickly assume the proportions of an international incident.

During the early days of his diagnosis in the hospital, we leaned heavily on each other for support, mentally and emotionally. We have a strong Christian faith and many supportive family members and friends, but when something like this happens, you do feel isolated, as if no one can possibly understand what you are going through or what you are feeling. Thankfully, we turned to each other and I believe our relationship grew stronger but it was by no means easy. It felt oddly like it was us against the world. Of course it wasn't, as so many people were there only too willing to help us, but that's how it felt.

Chapter 16

When we brought Matthew home, despite the devastating prognosis, we were both optimistic for a miracle and prepared to do everything we could to optimise his chances. However, in the day to day working out of that, we had no comprehension of how tiring that would be, or how angry, disappointed, sad and emotional we would feel. We were both working as hard as we could but with little proactive professional input and encouragement from the medical profession. As far as they were concerned, we had brought our son home to make him as comfortable as possible until he died, which they predicted would be sooner rather than later.

One advantage nursing our son at home afforded us was more freedom to care for him than we had in hospital. If we did not think it appropriate for him to be disturbed, that decision was not challenged. We dictated the daily schedules and I believe we undertook his care with his best interests at heart because we were able to give him two-to-one nursing. Home also gave us more freedom with each other to express our thoughts. Without other people around to overhear us we were able to speak our minds. We tried hard not to say anything that might cause Matthew undue stress, whilst also attempting to be honest with him, but it was often difficult and another measure of stress for us to deal with.

Even though he was still having strong anti-seizure drugs with sedative effects, we knew that when he was lucid, he could hear and understand everything that was being said. We also tried not to disagree or argue with each other in Matt's presence, as we felt it would be counterproductive. That said, exhausted through a huge sleep deficit and having changed bed linen for the umpteenth time and eventually sitting down to eat something at ten thirty in the evening, it was almost impossible to remain cool, calm and collected.

I now know my husband is an exceptional man. He has not only managed to endure this devastating time, but also all that I have thrown his way, and still love me despite everything. Mark and I have argued with each other more times than I care to admit within these pages. We have shouted at each other and ourselves in frustration and, I am ashamed to confess, we have even slapped each other when things became too much to take anymore. It is interesting that much of what stirred us to breaking point was often trivial – like changing bed linen or giving supplements in the wrong order. When it came to making decisions of major importance we were seldom so rattled or in disagreement.

All this highlights a valid point, that however strong your relationship is with someone, whatever life-shattering situations you may share and come through, stress of this kind needs an outlet. Each of us needed space to deal with our feelings. We were virtual prisoners in our own home, looking after our son under devastating circumstances. I remember reading 'The Diary of Anne Frank' as a child and wondering what on earth it must have felt like to be trapped indoors with other people for an extended time, never being allowed out. I now know and my heart aches for people in similar situations. At least I had someone to share everything with – the work, the fears, the heartache. There are many not so fortunate, who have to survive alone.

Many of the treatments and supplements we gave Matthew were really on a trial and error basis. We gained limited knowledge in a short time, but were far from qualified in such things as diet, nutrition and sickness. We made many contacts during those early months at home, mostly by word of mouth, as well as having access to a plethora of internet information. One particular friend, Ko Chohan, a leading advocate of natropathic nutrition, made time in her busy schedule to visit us and offer personal advice and aid in our alternative approach to Matt's illness. She confirmed our belief that the body's immune system needs to be maintained at peak performance levels for any chance of survival from degenerative disease.

On leaving hospital we mentioned we would be investigating alternative treatments, but received little enthusiasm and were frankly discouraged from pursuing that road. That was disheartening, as most people in our position would continue to fight to help their child against all the odds and invariably consider all possibilities. More than once we felt it would be wonderful to know the conventional medical profession was rooting for us, if not actively assisting. But if I am honest, most of what we attempted was not viewed with encouragement or enthusiasm. It seemed that a death sentence had been pronounced over our son and no allowances were made for any deviation from their predicted outcome.

I know many people would question alternative therapies for cancer, preferring instead conventional chemotherapy, radiotherapy and surgery, but I think it is a pity more alternative therapy is not offered alongside all of that. Having been advised no further conventional treatments would be of help to Matthew we were, within sensible reason, prepared to consider all other options. After much research, reading and prayer, and in addition to all his immune-boosting supplements and freshly prepared juices, we gave Matthew a course of B17 injections, which is derived from apricot kernels, and included powdered shark cartilage in his diet amongst other things.

Many claims have been made about certain products and there are those who would support their use and those who would not. Matthew's case was uncommon in that the diagnosis he had been given was rare. Melanoma is primarily a skin cancer that can invade (metastasise to) other parts of the body, with devastating speed. With no signs of it on his skin we were told that the tumour on the brain was the primary site. We had no guidelines by which to proceed, we had only our trust in God and our instincts and with hindsight, we would still have tried all that we did in the fight for our son's life. Everyone has his or her own decisions to make in situations like these and people can offer advice and help, but ultimately, as Matt's parents, it was for us to decide. That responsibility is not an easy thing to bear and we were frankly scared, deliberating long and hard over every choice.

Chapter 17

A midst all the busyness of Matt's care, we tried to find time to sit with him quietly everyday, reading to him or just talking. We had not done normal family things for ages, so we were both pleasantly surprised one evening when, facing towards the patio doors, he pointed with his moveable hand, behind him to the television on the opposite side of the room. An old James Bond movie was showing. Matt had always been a fan; he especially liked the cars and when we asked him if he wanted to be turned to watch it, he nodded, with a slight smile chasing around his lips. He looked like our Mattie. Our spirits soared as we realised our son was very much with us.

A particularly nasty problem we constantly battled with was the mucus that collected in Matthew's throat. It is a common thing in patients who are confined to bed. For Matt it was aggravated by the feeding tube down his nose and throat. We lived in continual fear of him suffering additional seizures because he could not breathe and we were forced to make frequent use of the suction machine for that problem. That in itself was a mixed blessing; the intrusion and noise of the apparatus in his throat or nose would cause him a great deal of stress which could also induce a seizure. We were caught between a rock and a hard place.

We held our breath and crossed off the weeks on the calendar. July came and went as England enjoyed some idyllic warm, sunshine-filled days. We received practical help and gifts from so many friends and neighbours, and members of our church. It was not unusual to open our front door and discover wonderful home-grown organic produce or beautiful flowers on the step. And cards and letters of encouragement kept flooding in.

Kind well-wishers from a nearby church gave us some money for Matt and we spent it on an awning, urgently needed to shade the patio and Matthew's bed space. We longed to be outside with him, but it was impossible with all the electrical paraphernalia that was constantly required for his care. We satisfied ourselves with the uplifting blue and white shading, cool fans blowing and the gentle fragrances of summer wafting in through wide open doors.

Although the doctors had said that the seizures would increase in frequency as his condition worsened, it was several weeks after returning home before one even occurred. It was almost a relief when it happened, although we didn't want him to suffer the fitting, but at least we then knew we could cope alone and thankfully without having to administer serious sedatives.

Matthew had lost a considerable amount of weight, probably about two stone since the onset of his illness, but looked remarkably healthy for a very sick young man. His hair had begun growing back, much darker than before, and his eyelashes and expressive eyebrows showed no signs of the ravages his body had endured. By now, newsletters that we sent out periodically to friends, were being circulated around the world. More and more people were joining with us to pray for Matt's recovery. In spite of setbacks, we were encouraged by the signs and we too kept hoping and praying.

In late August 2001, when it seemed Matthew was doing so well, he suffered a major setback contracting a serious infection in the Hickman Line in his chest. Hickman Lines can and do become infected and they are then often removed to reduce further risks. It is usually a straightforward procedure, if the patient is mobile and able to communicate. Our son was neither. He was still paralysed down his left-hand side and unable to speak. We were advised by the doctors that Matthew would need to return to hospital for antibiotics or line removal to eliminate the bugs.

Emotions were running high as Mark and I, constantly tired and easily frustrated, were confronted by this particularly difficult situation and as Matt's guardians we desperately wanted to do what was best for him. With a terminal diagnosis on leaving hospital, we had promised Matt that he would not have to return for more treatment. Whatever happened, we believed then that we would be able to keep that promise. It perhaps sounds like an odd thing to say but we felt very pressured to comply with this new suggested route of treatment.

Having diagnosed Matthew's condition as untreatable and terminal and admitting they could do no more for him they had allowed us to bring him home to nurse him until, according to their predictions, he died. Now they were trying to impress upon us the urgency of returning him to hospital for treatment as this present infection was life-threatening. However, we believed the only solution they offered could cause him serious stress that may also prove to be life-threatening. It was a very difficult dilemma. We talked, hugged and sobbed in our kitchen beyond Matthew's hearing, or so we thought, and after agonising deliberation and prayer, we dug our heels in and requested that he be treated at home.

The infection in his line was very serious and the doctors wanted to prescribe antibiotics before the test results were known. However, with uncharacteristic boldness, we asked them to delay until the results came back from the laboratory. With hindsight, it was the right choice as the tests revealed the superbugs in Matt's line to be a particularly aggressive strain and not known to respond to the usual drugs. However, miraculously it would seem, three months earlier a new antibiotic had been approved for use that was specifically tailored to the bugs in Matt's line. We didn't much like the idea of antibiotics but we had little choice and less time.

After entreating the doctors, they finally agreed to give him the antibiotics at home. It meant extra work for them but, to give them their due, once the decision was made they pulled out all the stops. The new drug arrived almost hot off the press, as it were and Matthew was given the antibiotics twice a day for the following two weeks.

My married sister had come to stay with us that month. Abandoning her own family to come and help care for mine, her presence was a huge stabilising influence on us all during those very painful days. She was Matt's number one fan and they had always enjoyed a close relationship although she lived some distance away. Jackie, or Auntie-in-Your-Face as she was lovingly referred to as she was always after a kiss or three, is incurably funny and always insisted on spoiling our son whenever she laid eyes on him. Thankfully she more than ably looked after Matt at that time while we discussed what to do in another room.

Calamitously, all the tension in the house proved too much for Mattie. Jackie realised he was aware Mark and I were disturbed by all the decisions we had to make and it had a traumatic effect on him. He began a series of seizures that escalated to a point where we had to call our local doctor in during the night and Matt was given seriously high doses of sedatives.

When he finally fell into a drugged sleep after two

frightening days of protracted seizures, his respiration was severely subdued and it was touch and go whether he would survive either the seizures or the sedatives. Unable and unwilling to sleep we kept yet another harrowing bedside vigil, joined by loving friends, praying and watching our son once more bravely fighting for his life. Miraculously, he slowly began to show signs of recovery as the line infection cleared without the need to return to hospital and we once more resumed life gingerly walking on eggshells.

Chapter 18

Because of the severity of Matt's condition and the intensity of our schedule, we took little notice of life outside our living room as we were virtually kept occupied all day and most of the night looking after our son. He was so very precious to us and our lives literally revolved around his bedside. That is until September 11th 2001, or 9/11 as it is now referred to. Unable to go out into the world, that day the world brutally crashed into our living room through the television screen. With countless others we watched, horrified, the unfolding events of destruction that wreaked havoc in so many lives.

Our own lives, together with our hopes and dreams, were abruptly arrested that night in April when Matthew was rushed to hospital. Life as we knew it was on indefinite hold. It was agonising to witness his illness and we experienced so much pain during those early months. But deep within that pain, we discovered a joy and love that we may otherwise have missed without the opportunity to focus on minute details of each other. Our hearts went out to all those people who lost loved ones in the tragedy in America. That precious time with our son filled us with memories that will ever quicken our hearts. For so many grieving families, the suddenness of their loss was perhaps the hardest emotion to come to grips with.

Aware that he could hear perfectly well and understand most things, we spoke to Mattie about those terrible events in the weeks that followed. We seemed to be living in a world gone crazy, where children get sick with deadly diseases and innocent lives are blown apart in the name of so-called religion, justice and revenge. We clung to our strong faith as we wept and prayed for everyone affected that, through disaster, fear and hopelessness, healing would come to those victims of September 11th. Meanwhile, our personal battle raged on. Living through it was a bizarre mixture of joy and thankfulness, pain and desperation.

All too often we seemed to go two steps forward and three back. Frustratingly, Matt's essential mineral levels rose and fell and he endured countless transfusions in an attempt to stabilise them. I think they failed because the transfusions were blitzing Matthew's body with synthetic substitutes. What our bodies need is a good balanced diet to provide all our nutrients in a natural way. Once we stopped the artificial chemical supplements, his levels seemed to improve and we witnessed outward signs that spoke of a body trying to heal itself. But juxtaposed with those strides forward, he was still physically sick most days, which was in itself debilitating and the mucus still caused him discomfort day and night. What is remarkable is that, during all that time, Matthew allowed us to do everything necessary for his care without ever complaining, even visually.

Although we sometimes had help from friendly volunteers at night, Mark and I continued to undertake the majority of Matt's twenty-four hour nursing needs but it's not something I would necessarily recommend. With hindsight, I would cease with my attempts to be superwoman and humbly accept offers of help more readily. Mark remained far more gentle spirited than me and looking back I can see that our different strengths and weaknesses compensated and complemented each other. One thing I do know is that we are stronger, encouraged, more determined people as a result of our experiences.

It would be easy to skim over all the bad days and simply tell everyone how well we handled those exhausting months at home, but believe me when I say the reality was not like that. Hurdle after hurdle found me sadly unable to clear the jumps without complaining, crying, begging God to do something, blaming myself or Mark and ending up in a crumpled heap, saying sorry to everyone and hating myself for being so weak. I know Mark had his own personal struggles, but he handled them differently and seldom burdened everyone else with them. He internalised much of what he felt; I continued to verbalise my feelings. My husband is no saint, but I'm totally grateful that he was there with me. His strength bolstered me up when I had all but thrown in the towel. When I cried and cried because I couldn't face anymore, it was Mark who lifted my chin and told me I could because both he and Matt needed me and couldn't survive without little ol' volatile me!

We were careful to try to eat well and sleep whenever we had an opportunity, but it was almost impossible to relax! As we ticked off more precious weeks on the calendar, we held our breath as the deadline for the prognosis passed. Friends came and camped at our house to ensure we celebrated Mark's birthday and our wedding anniversary in mid-September. The paradox was that we managed to eat home-made cake and drink some bubbly amidst the sick dishes and sheet changes! It brought a wry smile to Matthew's face when I told him just how old his Dad was. He didn't say anything, but I imagine he was thankful his Mum was so young!!!

On the speaking front, Matt was trying hard to communicate with us. He was using his right index finger to point a lot and managed to say quite a few words. On one particular occasion I had my hand on his head as I told him he was so beautiful, to which he tentatively affirmed, "So beau-ti-ful." Fortunately he was used to seeing me display my emotions, so I didn't feel a need to hold back the tears.

Though showing no actual movement in his left-hand side Mark and I thought his right arm and leg seemed stronger. With his good side, he began to move quite actively, so much so it became like trying to nurse a one-sided octopus. He wouldn't keep still when I did 'mumsy' sort of things either, like straighten his eyebrows or clean his ears, and I was amazed how a chap so disabled could still manage to be so stubborn when it came to teeth-cleaning and general hygiene!

Chapter 19

The days flew past in a constant flurry of nursing, feeding, researching and administering many different nutrients and supplements but we never seemed to have enough time to achieve all that we hoped. Mark had learnt how to change Matt's feeding tube, which meant we were not dependent on professional nursing cover for such emergencies, but often our tenuous schedule would be completely blown away by a morning of sickness and the suction machine or an emergency tube change and we would remain in our pyjamas well into the afternoon. Outside, the world continued to turn, yet our attention was focused intently on the inert body of our only child. I often wanted to run outside and berate passers-by for carrying on with their lives so unaware of our trials.

Looking back through our diaries to write this, I am amazed at how much our lives seesawed from one extreme to another and how we kept going. It seemed that we barely had more than a day of stability before something would present itself as a setback. And yet, at the time, despite the repetitive sickness, mucus, diarrhoea, seizures and endless nursing, the overwhelming sense our diary entries convey is one of hope – that Matt was progressing towards life not death.

I was never more aware that we must live in the present moment and neither look back to what was, or forward to what might be, than when I read a moral tale about a monk being pursued by a ferocious tiger:

"The monk raced to the edge of the cliff, glanced back, and saw the growling tiger about to spring. The monk spotted a rope dangling over the edge of the cliff. He grabbed it and began shinning down the side of the cliff out of the clutches of the tiger. Whew! Narrow escape. He stared down and saw a huge quarry of jagged rocks five hundred feet below. He looked up and saw the tiger poised on top of the cliff with bared claws. Just then, two mice began to nibble at the rope.

The monk saw a strawberry within arm's reach growing out of the face of the cliff side. He plucked it, ate it, and exclaimed,'Yum yum: that's the best strawberry I've ever tasted in my entire life.' If he had been preoccupied with the rock below (the future) or the tiger above (the past), he would have missed the strawberry God was giving him in the present moment. Moral of the story: Do not focus on the tigers of the past or the impossible rocks of the future, but only on the strawberry that comes in the here and now."

During one such volatile week, our precious darling son suffered so badly from sickness – to the point where he kept little sustenance down, even though it was administered in the purest form of freshly prepared juices. Conversely, his magnesium level rose for the third consecutive week without additional infusions! His tiny naso-gastric tube, the only means by which we could feed him and give oral medicines, had been causing his already sore throat great discomfort and then, by way of a change, he suffered severe constipation. Yet, the mucus and phlegm that had been dogging him for weeks seemed to be less aggressive. My diary entry that week read:

Yesterday – the tiger:
After a fraught weekend of constipation, followed by copious sheet changes and sick bowls up to our elbows, I was standing inside my wardrobe (a quirky habit I have when the pressure

gets too much) trying to decide whether it would be worth changing into fresh clothes again that day. I felt as if I couldn't go on any more because as soon as one thing was dealt with another issue leapt up to take its place. No sooner had I finished moaning loudly in the wardrobe that all we needed was an even break, than it dawned on me that actually our prayers were being answered. Matthew had come home, the fits were not increasing, magnesium levels were improving, mucus did seem to be lessening, and so on.

Tomorrow – the rocks:

Believing that Matthew is going to get well is the biggest test of my faith and I am sure of Mark's too. It is hard for our finite minds to understand how on earth Matt can recover from such a complicated and devastating illness. How will all his wasted muscles regain their former strength? How will he speak again? How will his left side move again? The doctors have diagnosed such and such – how on earth can he ever recover? Well, in the wardrobe yesterday, I decided I'd try not to worry about any of that – but to concentrate on the here and now. The unique irreplaceable present.

Today – the strawberry!

Today, I didn't give anything else a thought, except what a privilege it is to be here with my husband, nursing and loving our precious son. A neighbour came to read to him from the 'The Lion, the Witch and the Wardrobe' and I hung around on the periphery performing unimportant little chores, like folding sheets, just listening too and watching everything about our son. And then it came – the strawberry. Matthew smiled at me, the biggest broadest smile I have seen for many a long month – for no reason – and my heart melted. Yum yum, that was the best smile I've ever seen in my whole life! And today, for the first time in weeks and weeks, Matthew was not sick. Thank you God.

It's difficult to verbalise the hope we felt in those post-prognosis months at home. On the face of it, everything we had been told in connection with his diagnosis spelt doom and gloom. We had after all been advised that there was nothing more medically that could be done for him and our expectations were certainly not raised beyond looking after our son for a short time until he died. I know our strength and the ability to carry on day after day came from our Christian faith but, like most parents, there was a tenacity in both of us that refused to stop until we had exhausted every avenue in an attempt to change the forecast. It helped to have a vision, to believe that Matthew would recover from this terrible illness. But for that vision to remain alive, we had to focus on short-term goals. We had to set small targets and strive to meet them, otherwise the vastness of the whole picture could seem overwhelming. As I had written in my journal, "Focus on the present."

Chapter 20

One such goal was to have a physiotherapist visit and initiate some proactive rather than palliative care. On our instigation fortnightly visits were eventually arranged and we discovered that although Matt had a lot of wasted muscle, there was still a degree of flexibility in all his joints. Mark learned the gruelling exercises and incorporated those into our already overstretched schedule.

Again, at our insistence, a speech therapist was also consulted and came up with some good ideas for us to work on to encourage Matthew to speak again and we had extra input from professional friends eager to help stimulate his brain. We put some great pictures onto a board with velcro and other generous friends donated a brand new laptop to Matthew, complete with a wire-less mouse in the hope that he could be taught to manoeuvre it himself. Mark dug out an oversized Connect 4 game and spent precious time playing with Matt. Somehow, even guiding Matthew's hand with the counters, Mark still managed to lose, but it was worth his humiliation just to see the two of them together in a precious cameo of our past life.

Every miniscule movement was a gigantic effort for Matt so we were always ecstatic when he spoke or gestured to us. We were bowled over when he said haltingly, "I don't like that flavour," as I was cleaning his dry mouth and lips with a glycerine-moistened sponge. Mark and I nearly fell over with shock. The speech therapist explained that type of sentence is an automatic response and not to get too excited about it – but it was too late, we got excited. We didn't care if it was automatic, manual, premeditated, spontaneous combustion or whatever – our son had spoken a sentence!

Just before Matt's illness, Mark decided to transplant a beautiful tree from our back garden to the front. Not too scary a proposition, unless you are the tree! Unlike Dr Christian Barnard, Mark does not have a good track record transplanting. For a brief time it looked truly wonderful outside our study window at the front of the house. But sadly it was neglected during our hospital stay and when we came home it was all brown and looked to all intents and purposes to be dead.

Faithful friends tended our garden after our return home which gave us much pleasure during our confinement to barracks. But the tree seemed beyond help – that was until one day, amongst the barren branches, a tiny splash of green was observed. That new life clung on against all the odds and our tree survived. We likened it to our son who, after being home for some eighteen weeks, had beautiful new hair covering his head and splashes of colour in his cheeks!

We had Matthew measured up for a specialist wheelchair with head supports. We felt it would be so good for him to be wheeled into other rooms in the house as we had all been trapped in our lounge for too long. The National Health Service couldn't promise that we would receive it in time, but our dream was for him to sit with us at the table in the kitchen for Christmas lunch 2001, eight months after he had become ill. I prayed with Matt that his chair would also be trendy – motorised if possible – and adjustable for several positions. The hopes and dreams we nurtured in our hearts kept us going as winter pushed autumn out of the picture frame and the rich golden tones in our garden gave way to barren branches and bleak, grey days.

By the time mid-November hit town, the weather seemed all too soon to consist of dark evenings and the need for warmer clothes. Rain, biting winds and thermal underwear were once again on the agenda. After two months in hospital wards, watching the sun beat down on our concrete prison, we had swapped that incarceration to briefly glimpse blue skies and sunshine through the glass of our patio doors. Now, with the onset of another winter, we felt as if we were being robbed of time.

Matthew had bypassed two whole seasons' clothes and looked set to outgrow everything in his wardrobe. The last time he stood up he was eyeballing my 5'4" frame. When a friend and I measured him as best we could in his bed he had easily passed that landmark. The closest idea we had of how much he had grown was when his rapidly sprouting friends visited. Mark and I were made aware of the young man where once the boy lay and realised how privileged we were to witness all the intimate changes accompanying that.

As we all grew older, it made me think how much in life is taken for granted. Like most people, if I'm honest, serious life-threatening illness was not something I had budgeted for, certainly not for my child anyway. I would always pray that Matt wouldn't take drugs, get knifed, or even contract Aids, but though we are bombarded with statistics predicting one in three people will develop cancer in their lifetime, it was never something I thought would happen to us. It was always something that happened to other people, sometimes to people I knew, but not to me, nor my husband and certainly not my son.

During those times we were all together at home, we looked at each day as a self-contained unit and thanked

God for what we most graciously had that millions did not, for the fact that we were alive and loved each other and didn't live in a country ravaged by war. That we were not starving, or physically or sexually abused. It made me realise that we can do too much planning for our own and our children's possible future, trying to pre-empt too many scenarios. My point is, do we fully appreciate every second we have and make it count for something? Do you know there are 86,400 seconds in each day? No pressure, as they say, just think about them. Someone sent us this quote:

"Imagine there is a bank that credits your account each morning with £86,400. It carries over no balance from day to day. Every evening it deletes whatever part of the balance you failed to use during the day.

What would you do each day? Draw out every penny, of course!!!"

Chapter 21

It was exciting when we took delivery of the wheelchair for Matt in plenty of time for Christmas, but that was short-lived as we quickly realised it was not the specialist type we had asked for and was totally inadequate. However we were asked to try it out before returning it but that proved disastrous as Matthew was uneasy with the hoist used to transfer him and, because the wheelchair wasn't suitable, it proved an extremely stressful episode for him and he ended up having a series of seizures. With hindsight I would have gone with my initial gut feeling about the chair and declined the trial. Some things you learn the hard way.

Apparently, a minute's seizure is like running a mile. That particular series of seizures lasted a total of nine minutes over four hours! We put it down to painful experience and ordered another wheelchair, hopeful that once we were able to place Matt in a suitable one for even a few minutes a day, it would help his body clear the mucus from his throat. We all hated using the inadequate and noisy suction machine. Its drawbacks in Matt's situation far outweighed its usefulness.

We had devised several positions and angles in his bed that we used for Matt everyday, changing him about every two hours. But even so, he was immobile by any standards and whenever we attempted to imitate his positions for very long, our limbs suffered from pins and needles and our bodies hastily screamed out for change – not an option for Matthew. It was extremely difficult and emotionally draining, nursing someone who could not speak. Much of what we did for him to make him comfortable was guesswork on our part. Very occasionally, he would nod or shake his head to indicate his preferences, but mostly he declined to interact in that area. I don't know whether it was because he couldn't always answer, whether it was too difficult for him or whether he simply did not choose to; either way it made for frequent frustration for all of us I think.

Simple things like washing Matt's hair was a procedure requiring the skill and precision timing of a military operation. We finally secured a device that resembled a tiny blow-up swimming pool but lower on one of its four sides. We had to manoeuvre that underneath his head, whilst he lay flat on the bed. Then with copious saucepans of tepid water and jugs, we would wet, wash and rinse his hair. The excess water was supposed to run out through a tube into a bowl or bucket in place for the purpose. Well that was the theory anyway. The reality was usually another sheet change and a time of great stress for us all and, although not a frequent necessity, it was still another risky chore to be undertaken. Often it would precipitate small seizures and we only did it when we had to. Similarly cutting Matt's once-more prolific hair, to minimise his discomfort when we moved his head, was a task none of us looked forward to, and had to be tackled with extreme care and dexterity.

Although certain help was available through the National Health Service in the United Kingdom, because Matt's progress had not gone according to the predictions of the medical profession, Mark and I felt very much alone in caring for our son, boldly going where no one had gone before – or no one we knew and could consult anyway. The setbacks and crises when they did happen were usually at night, all adding to the tension. It is a huge and frightening responsibility to try to prevent your child from possibly choking to death in the middle of the night on secretions he cannot clear from his throat. There's something about experiencing suffering in this way that sharpens your awareness of the sufferings of others. In a world where man's inhumanity to man is rampant, all three of us were deeply aware of our blessings and nurtured a desire to help others. At that time our family prayers were always for an end to the terrible suffering of countless others in the world as well as our own.

December came and we battled on undertaking all of Matt's care, desperately in need of more help yet unsure of how we might achieve that. Then, in answer to prayer, we were introduced through our community nurse to a lovely trainee nurse called Michelle, who was able to supplement her hours by being with us for a few hours every week. It was possible for her to earn considerably more in the private sector, but she chose to forego financial gain to bless our family. She was tailor-made for Matt – young, lively, and with a mean CD collection. It afforded Mark and I a little respite to do other things around the house, whilst assured that our son was well cared for. I know Matthew enjoyed those special times because his face would always light up when she arrived. Also, we were slowly being encouraged by the favourable results of the regular weekly blood tests, so even during that wintry December we saw promising horizons of joyful hope.

Although Matt was still experiencing seizures, their duration and severity still did not seem to be worsening as had been forecast. Coupled with the extended time beyond the prognosis that he had been at home and his renewed attempts at speaking, it was understandable that our hope remained buoyant despite all the bad days. His most welcome attempts to chat seemed more prominent during the night. I actually had to put my finger to his lips while changing him once, as Mark was taking advantage of a stable night and grabbing some rare shut-eye upstairs and Matt was making a good attempt at calling out loud. I couldn't make out what it was he was trying to say, so I leaned over and put my ear close to his mouth and heard him quite clearly say "hug". A hug has always been the recognised panacea for all ills in our family so I quickly lay as close as I could on my bed next to his lowered air-filled machine and duly obliged. You can't let an opportunity like that slip by can you?

As the army of people who knew about Matthew and his incredible fight for life continually grew it was exciting to switch on the computer. We would sit by his bed with his laptop in front of him and read out all the messages, prayers and encouraging words of hope that were sent to him from around the world. Mark put out the word that Matthew was a discerning judge of jokes and invited anyone to submit their best ones for his scrutiny. I know there were several that earned Matt's approval and the arched eyebrow award. Some even made it as far as the inimitable half smile award that occasionally appeared.

Our lounge resembled a battle headquarters. Mark posted maps all over the walls opposite Matt's bed and stuck smiley faces on places where we had acquired new friends. We tacked colourful posters to the ceiling and suspended mobiles above his bed to provide interesting focal points for a young lad, forced to spend all day lying in bed, unable to speak properly or move by himself.

By now his health regime, modified and fine-tuned, had become an extremely complex affair. As a result of continual research, we were feeding him only freshly squeezed vegetable or fruit juices, all specifically chosen for their immune-boosting abilities and we ensured that everything he had was organically grown. Our food bill each week for his needs alone was in the region of sixty pounds. We had been fortunate in discovering a local farm shop that could supply all our needs. We were soon on first name terms with Sylvana, the remarkable lady who owned and ran the shop. She herself had recovered from cancer many years before and realising the importance of good nutrition, had opened her organic farm shop to help others.

Carrot juice was the mainstay of his diet in those early months. After we stopped giving him the standard prescribed milk feed we were giving him around twenty kilos of carrots each week, as well as vast amounts of apples and some beetroots. Matthew's skin looked remarkable. Weeks before he had exhibited numerous surface spots, especially on his face, but these had gone and his complexion was enviable by anyone's standards. We later learned that the pimples were probably signs of his body detoxifying through his skin, the body's largest organ, assisted by his diet and were not just due to his age and hormones, In fact, when a disease like cancer is present in the body, the immune system is so undermined it often fails to respond to external stimuli. One example was hay fever; Matt had regularly suffered each year, but since the onset of his illness there had been no outward manifestations of this allergy.

Chapter 22

A new, more suitable wheelchair arrived just in time for Christmas, but our excitement was again short-lived as we realised that Matthew wasn't really strong enough to sit in it at that time. His sleeping pattern had improved somewhat. At least by that December he wasn't spending every night wide awake staring ahead with a fearful look on his face, but he still faced daily discomfort and pain that would have defeated the strongest of us, and all without even the slightest murmur or moaning.

We were graced with a personal carol concert outside on our patio that December when a valiant group of singers from our church, including some very young ones, braved the cold night air and came to sing their hearts out for us. It was a special moment as we pulled back the curtains to reveal the glowing faces of those responsible for the lovely singing. Wrapping Matt in blankets and positioning his bed so that he could see, we opened the doors to admit the soft sounds of their voices. Our eyes filled with tears and thankfulness at their priceless gesture. We dispatched them later with mince pies and something warming!

On Christmas Eve a multitalented musical family of friends, lovingly referred to by us as the von Trapps, also stopped by to play and sing. Their unique gifts brought a smile to Matt's face and tears once again to the rest of us. We wanted Christmas to be a private affair just for the three of us and although there were countless family and friends who would gladly have given up their own plans to help us then, we chose to spend the time together quietly. We bought a few simple presents for Matt and each other and opened them, as we had always done before, in our beds all next to each other on Christmas morning.

We slept in our favourite positions, just like the three bears, with baby bear in the middle of two people who loved him more than they dare voice. Our hearts were breaking as we fought back tears and memories of other Christmases, when Matt had been well and the promise of halcyon days stretched endlessly into the future. Our vicar and others from Church came to share Communion with us that morning as we celebrated the 28th week of Matthew being home. It was a special time. He wasn't much interested in the presents, but visitors caught his attention and were rewarded with his inimitable arched eyebrow or a smile.

Unfortunately, the remainder of the day did not pan out as we had hoped. Unable to cope with the mucus in his throat, Matthew was very sick and Mark and I spent most of the the time cleaning him up, changing his sheets, crying silently and trying to make him as comfortable as we could. We finally ate our Christmas meal cold, on trays by his bedside, late that evening. We were totally exhausted, and wondered how long we could keep up such a relentless schedule but promising each other that this time next year things would be very different.

In the early hours of Boxing Day morning, as Mark and I got up to change Matt and turn him, we shivered in the cold. Outside the temperature had dropped below freezing. We hurried to finish our familiar routine and eagerly scrambled back under warm duvets, pausing too briefly to think about the people who were sleeping rough or on the streets that Christmas night. At least our son was with us and safe. Thankful for our home and abundant provisions we had been blessed with, we drifted into a brief though ever welcome rest.

December 30th 2001 was Matthew's thirteenth birthday. Family and friends came bearing gifts and helium balloons to hang around his bed. He received an incredible number of cards from well-wishers and we decorated our lounge with them as we poured out our love onto him, trying hard not to stifle him. Our boy was now thirteen, but he was and always would be my baby, my special guy. We tried hard not to think too much about how different life had been in the past, nor what it might be in the future. We sucked each drop of moisture out of this special anniversary. We probably kissed our son too much, held his hands too much and hugged him too much but he was after all our unique and darling boy and we considered ourselves very blessed that he was alive.

Chapter 23

Suddenly, miraculously, it was 2002 – a new year beginning. It was a very different beginning than any we had experienced before but, as weeks passed, we continued to cling to the hope that Matthew would get well. As I have said, it was our faith that sustained us during those long gruelling days and nights of caring for our son. Being Christians didn't give us all the answers, only a lot of questions. Believe me, we didn't spend all day being cheerful and endlessly energetic like Julie Andrews in 'The Sound of Music' and we didn't hover several feet above the ground with a Bible quotation for every situation. In truth, although we had our faith and hope for a better future, we still had to live out the daily twenty-four hour nitty-gritty and it was the toughest thing we'd ever done. But we did what any loving parents would do for their sick and suffering child, the very best we could do with the limited means and knowledge we had at our disposal.

Some people possess remarkable abilities to withstand torturous experiences and still maintain an incredible degree of calm. That was not the case for us. We battled every day to deal with our circumstances and align those with our faith in God. Many people have questioned whether the events in our lives threatened that faith. In all honesty, I would have to say 'no'. At no time did we doubt either the existence of God or the fact that He had the ability to change our circumstances. So why didn't He? I guess that would be one of the first questions I'd like an answer to. I understand that life on this earth is not fair, but God is still God. He doesn't promise to remove all the terrible things that exist in this world at the moment, they are the effects of the way our world chooses to live. He only promises to be with us no matter what we go through. And I truly believe He was with us, He is with us and He will always be with us, our Rock in times of trouble. We had to choose to trust that all things would be right one day, for everyone.

During that January, we were at last able to celebrate Matthew sitting in his wheelchair on two occasions. Unwilling to use the uncomfortable hoist in case it stressed him again, we discovered that it was a three-man operation requiring all the precision of positioning a reluctant driver into a Formula One car. But with a little help from friends – who called round at the drop of a hat – we did it! We didn't actually break any speed records gently pushing Matt across the lounge and along the hallway to the door of the kitchen, but we had great hopes in the boy's potential. More importantly, there were no apparent after-effects from those first tentative excursions.

Matthew remained pretty stable, though still paradoxically suffering badly some days from sickness, secretions, phlegm and seizures – but we were feeling much less fearful during any attacks. The more things we had to deal with, the more our confidence grew. He suffered from ingrown toenails, which seemed surprising as he had not worn shoes for ages, but an infection developed in his big toes and we had to seek professional help from a visiting chiropodist. It proved to be an extremely painful episode for Mattie but again he endured it all, although it did trigger a couple of seizures. Visitors always remarked how well he looked and Mark became joyfully aware of tiny movements on Matt's left-hand side, where none had been detected before.

We had occupied our house for less than a year when Matthew became ill, and although the packing-boxes had all miraculously been laid to rest, there lurked in nearly every corner, evidence that we had not completely made this abode our home. Cherished pictorial collages of our life still stood propped against largely unadorned walls, hoping for promotion to the spotlight.

After returning home from hospital we made a huge effort to hang all those fond memories around the house. Many of the photos shared a common theme – Matthew! It became important to have those reminders of our life together on constant view because the alternative, of happening unprepared upon a picture, was too painful an experience. We gave ourselves a pictorial history of his life to glance at fondly or linger over at leisure, should that rare occasion arise.

There is so much about my son that I treasure in my heart and I found myself more than willing to speak about him whenever I got the opportunity. A friend recently reminded me that I was asked to speak in our Church on Christmas Eve 2000 and I talked about relationships and loving our children. It also reminded me that Matthew was sitting, or rather draping himself over a chair as only adolescents can, in the second row of seats that day, listening. It's still not cool to sit at the front of anywhere before you're at least twenty-something! I sensed he outwardly felt a little embarrassed that I should use him for so many examples, but underneath he was thrilled to hear stories about himself. I am proud that he is my son and, secretly, I think he thought I was pretty much okay as a mum.

The times before our children move beyond our sphere of influence are special times. We do not create who they are, but we can help set them upon the path to where they want to go. We can form bonds with them that will show them unconditional acceptance and increase their self-esteem. We can discipline them to give them boundaries. We can give assurance of our love and support and above all be real with them, in successes and failures – admit when we get it wrong and ask their forgiveness when we need to. And we can pray that all these qualities will help them to be well-adjusted human beings with an acute awareness of the world around them. Mark and I can only hope that our amateur efforts made a difference. Our son was not perfectly behaved and beyond reproach. And Mark and I had not conquered the pitfalls of parenting; in fact often, even moderate success seemed a million miles away, but we were willing to improve.

Living through my pain during Matt's illness, I found it helped to recall and be so thankful for all the special times I had with my son, aware that there were never enough of those, but knowing some people are not so fortunate. Mark and I wished that we had taken more opportunities to be with him – to sit and watch a film with him without interruption, to listen more, to laugh with him more instead of nagging him to finish his homework, to move busy schedules around just to hang out with him before his tottering steps became a young man's independent strides. But in the depths of the dark nights I had to be content to treasure all those happy memories and ponder such things in my heart.

Only God knows our allotted time on this earth, but we can live each day as if it is our last. I know that sounds corny, as it has been said so often. But each extra day we had with Matt was more precious than the last, each moment treasured in our hearts. His sudden illness caused a sword to pierce my soul and will forever bear a scar, no matter how thorough the healing. We have our children's company exclusively for such a short time before we share them with their friends, spouses, careers, sickness and sometimes death, but the treasured memories stored up in our hearts can be dusted off and pondered any time at all. Before you go to sleep tonight, hug someone and tell them you love them – infinity and beyond!

Chapter 24

Throughout January, we continued with the diet of juices and supplements. It was not easy as we had to purchase items from so many different sources, some abroad, and it was a time-consuming affair requiring constant attention and review. But, encouragingly, Matt was now regularly sitting in his wheelchair for short periods of time and with some donated money we were able to secure the additional services of a private physiotherapist once a week.

The National Health Service provided Matthew with an hour of professional physiotherapy every four weeks, but the daily exercises still had to be undertaken by Mark. He was fantastic in all he achieved, but due to lack of any training he could only progress as far as each monthly visit would allow. The additional hour each week meant we were able to attempt more active exercises and assess Matt more frequently. We continued to encourage him to make sounds and attempt to speak, chatting to him about anything and everything. Occasionally our earnest efforts were richly rewarded.

January was also the month that we were truly blessed in the shape of some ministering angels! The Marie Curie Organisation is a charitable UK concern offering nursing help with cancer patients, including children which, incidentally, the Macmillan Nursing organisation doesn't cover. We were provided with overnight help three nights a week by the organisation. They funded half the costs and our local health council funded the other half. Their dedicated staff concentrate in specialised care for extremely disabling illnesses and referral is available through doctors' surgeries in England. So three gentle and devoted nurses came to our rescue. Each night one of them was with us it provided Mark and I with professional nursing support, as well as friendship and compassionate care, and meant so much in so many ways.

They would sit and watch Matt all night and we would take it in turns to sleep on a foldaway bed at the opposite end of the lounge, away from the noise of the air bed but providing essential back-up for changing and moving him. When surplus to requirements, Mark and I had the luxury of getting reacquainted with our bed for a whole night! It was wonderful, just knowing that two more-than-able bodies were on call should Matthew need them, and it enabled us both to catch up on some much-needed sleep and return refreshed the following morning, ready to carry on.

We became really close friends with our wonderful nurses, Olivia, Rhiannon and Heather, and added their office staff to our growing list of friends. They offered Matt and us so much love, above and beyond the requirements of their jobs. They spoiled us totally. And their timely arrival on the scene gave us strength to continue. We are eternally grateful for their selfless service, the gifts, cards, prayers and words of encouragement they brought into our home. Their services also released our family and friends from constantly worrying about us and freed up their time to assist us in other essential ways. Matthew seemed comfortable with them too and often showed his own appreciation with meaningful looks from his big expressive blue eyes as well as an occasional word or two!

Matt's friends visited him from time to time. Visiting in general wasn't always easy to arrange, as his condition was still volatile, but we encouraged them to see him if they could handle it – though I do not think it was an easy time for any of them. They knew Matthew as an extremely active person, full of life, and to learn of his illness was difficult. To actually see him, disabled and unable to speak was quite shocking and, I know, had a profound effect on them all.

One huge challenge we faced when his friends made the pilgrimage to our house was understanding that as teenagers they don't have to speak all the time, they can just hang out silently together, which they frequently did at Matt's bedside. What we had to do was just let them, making sure we remained open and approachable if they did suddenly feel like talking about what had happened.

Mattie's classmates at school diligently remembered him, creating a special place for him in all their joint projects. With the support of his form teacher, the headmaster and entire school, they creatively raised money to be used for his treatment. The fruits of their labour were staggering by any standards, but especially because their fund-raising was done out of real love for our son. Their regular contact and larger-than-life innovative cards kept us amused and made our lounge wallpaper infinitely more interesting.

Through the internet and useful advice, we decided we needed more hands-on professional help with Matthew's nutrition. With this in mind, I enrolled on a day's course that February to learn about a programme called the Gerson Therapy, which boasted some success with cancer patients balancing the body's complex chemistry with careful diet and supplements. Mark remained at home with willing volunteers and I spent the day locally, learning all I could about this particular therapy and applying it to Matt.

Most of the other people attending the course were either cancer patients or carers and the day was informative and encouraging in that it afforded an opportunity to ask lots of questions, share your experiences and fears and listen to others in various stages of the disease. It made me realise once again that cancer is no respecter of persons. You can be rich or poor, old or young, but like so many of the degenerative illnesses that attack our immune systems, cancer seems too often to wear the victor's crown.

With hindsight, it is our hope that through sharing our knowledge gained on the hoof, we will be able to open up more choices and real options for others dealing with this illness. Despite great medical and scientific breakthroughs we still have much to learn about our bodies and how we can best treat them to prevent so much disease. Many fellow sufferers of cancer, forced to evaluate their lifestyles, decide to change them completely, but others make no such alterations. It is all about choice or, in Matthew's case, the best choice we could make on his behalf.

As it turned out, because Matt's case was extremely rare with unusual complications, it was necessary for us to modify the Gerson programme for him and that in itself seemed to defeat the object of the therapy, since its success relied much on strict adherence to the regime. Also at that time there were a limited number of doctors overseeing this treatment in the UK, thereby requiring patients to visit them at their busy practices. As Matthew was unable to travel we couldn't really avail ourselves of this particular treatment but we did incorporate many of the principals into our care plan for him. Because his condition was not deteriorating according to the prognosis of the medical profession we knew that something of what we were doing was achieving varying levels of change. What we did not know was what and how much.

With our newly acquired though limited knowledge we continued to give Matt the freshest juices, all organic, together with a cocktail of supplements, alongside several other more unusual ingredients in the hope that some or all of them would boost his own body's immune system. However, without structured professional guidance it was rather a hit and miss affair. Although we did not feel these treatments were exorbitantly expensive we were still fortunate to have a steady donation of money to fund this and we were acutely aware that without such support our modest savings would have been quickly swallowed up. We were blessed with an incredible network of loving family, friends and strangers. But we were only too aware that many people in similar circumstances do not have those advantages.

Mark writes:
Due mainly to lack of manpower, our National Health Service was only able to provide physiotherapy every four weeks at home. It is usually expected that home carers will learn the exercises and supplement the treatment. All the workouts were essential for Matt and so I got stuck in and learned as many as I could and I would give him physio every day. I felt inadequate really, as I could only go as far as I had been taught, but at least I felt useful and it proved to be a special time for my son and me. We would look at each other's faces closely during those sessions, speaking only with our eyes it seemed. It was never a chore for me as I knew it was a necessity to keep Matt's body from stiffening up from such a long time in bed and it was an extension of the intense love I felt for my son. I didn't want to hurt him but knew I had to push on with it if he was ever going to be able to walk again. The more supple I helped him to be, the less he would need splints or casts in the future. When we were able to afford some extra private physio it helped me, complementing what we were already doing and brought some fresh input to Matt's exercise regime.

Because he had been left partially paralysed after the biopsy and unable to speak, it was quite difficult to gauge how much he could comfortably bear, so I would always maintain eye contact to read his expressions whilst encouraging his limbs to go to the limits of their ability. Characteristically he would try to resist me with his right side as he had some strength there, but there was no resistance at first from his left limbs. Knowing how active he had always been, it inevitably brought tears to my eyes to see his inert little body lying there with those trusting eyes just looking up to me, his dad. Only God knows what questions he wanted to ask; I could only pray God answered them for my boy. With unspoken teamwork, we slowly made what seemed like snail's progress, but in view of how ill he was and what he had endured, they were milestones in anyone's book. I was so proud of him.

Chapter 25

Although Matthew looked physically more healthy on the surface than he had for a long time, there were several things that concerned us and about which we continued to seek advice and help. He was still having large amounts of anti-seizure medication, based on his original prescription. As he continued to outlive the doctors' forecast quite considerably, we became concerned about the possible side-effects from long-term use of that class of drug. It is possible to research information about prescription drugs fairly easily on the internet and what we learned disturbed us: that the side-effects might now outweigh the benefits. So we discussed the possibility of reducing them.

The medical profession were reluctant to do this as they felt the consistently high levels of drugs, prescribed originally according to his weight, were still required to prevent Matt's seizures – even though he had by then lost considerable weight. Also what Mark and I were observing in constant close proximity to Matthew was that the seizures he was experiencing had changed both in pattern and duration.

It appeared to us that they manifested when he was particularly stressed about something or unable to communicate his thoughts, and we began to question whether they were now caused by pressure on his brain from an enlarging tumour at all. The force of them had altered considerably and, whereas initially Matt seemed unconscious throughout, he now appeared to remain aware of his surroundings during a seizure and often only small areas of his body were affected. We put any decision about this on hold for a while longer and observed him ever more closely.

Slowly we were gaining insight into the dangerous equation during the lead up to Matthew's body becoming sick. One vital part of that discovery was his eating preferences, which pre-illness had caused us some concern. We didn't feel we had received enough education and guidance as parents to the dangerous consequences of some childrens' diets. Many of the things we were learning set alarm bells ringing. As a fussy eater for much of his latter years he didn't eat overly much, but with hindsight we realised much of what he did eat not only didn't provide him with balanced nutrition, but could have harmful consequences.

Unlike many of his peers Matt ate little obvious junk food. He chose to eat very little meat, seldom fish, unless it was processed and disguised with batter or bread crumbs, eggs if disguised and pasta, rice and vegetables under duress. A weekly treat of pizza swallowed down with mayonnaise was probably his favourite meal. And whereas we were happy he was not a tomato ketchup addict, he acquired such a fondness for mayonnaise, now believed to be carcinogenic, that found him reaching for it whenever he was allowed. Feeding him what I considered to be nutritious food had become a struggle and we inevitably left the battlefield thankful that he had eaten anything! Along with many other children, Matthew was a child of the processed food era.

Through our research we discovered that oils heated in preparation, whether partially or fully hydrogenated, and found in an endless list of ready-prepared foods as well as margarine, spreads, chocolate and sauces are harmful to us. Hydrogenation, the most common and cheapest way of changing natural oils for human consumption, provides cheap products, but in the process destroys any benefits and forms substances that contain remnants of nickel and aluminium that our bodies cannot break down and are proving to be directly linked to many modern day diseases.

We knew that oils are essential to life and good health, but were only now learning about those specific oils and their particular forms. Trans-fatty acids, for instance, present in large quantities in hydrogenated products are harmful – but we need to know the difference between good and bad oils so that we can make intelligent choices about our diet, rather than throwing the baby out with the bath water as recently courted low-fat diets seem to advocate. But countless food manufacturers want us simply to buy their products, with little information about how they are manufactured.

Matthew seldom if ever drank plain water preferring fruit juices and artificially-sweetened cordials. We did not allow him to have flavoured sodas, in an attempt to avoid too much refined sugar which again is harmful to our bodies. However, in the search to create chemical substitutes for sugar that do not contain excessive calories, we have created a chemical monster in the shape of artificial sweeteners that too are known to be carcinogenic. Subsequently, countless parents allow their children to consume vast quantities of artificially-sweetened drinks, believing they are preferable.

Matt would eat home-made soups if pureed and he liked yoghurts, though mostly flavoured and again artificially-sweetened ones. Potatoes were often the mainstay of his meal, either baked or mashed, but he declined to eat the beneficial skin, and he loved cheese, especially cooked, another thing we are now advised to eat in moderation. To many this cocktail is not necessarily threatening, but we discovered to our horror that some constitutions are more predisposed to certain illnesses than others and our diet plays no small part in how our bodies cope with disease. What you feed your body has a direct influence on its ability and speed to recognise and destroy malignant cell formation.

Despite expressing our concern as he grew between the ages of six and twelve, we were reassured by family doctors that although big in size and weight for his age Matt was not considered obese and his weight would probably adjust itself in his adolescent years. Certainly, as he developed he seemed very similar to his father who had appeared quite chubby until he was twelve. Of course, in a lot of cases, this is the pattern of growth and there is nothing sinister about a degree of chubbiness before children mature but the gift lies in being able to distinguish the crucial difference in each individual. Now of course we are being bombarded with information that confirms a frightening percentage of children in western civilisations are overweight, even to the extent of being obese.

Sadly we are given vastly conflicting and constantly changing messages about what is and isn't beneficial for us to eat, whilst being coerced to consume increasing amounts of refined, processed and genetically modified foods and chemical substitutes for the real thing. With media advertising, changing lifestyles and busy schedules where family mealtimes are eroded away, it has become increasingly difficult to encourage children to eat a balanced diet. Too late, we are being advised of many foods to be avoided, whilst inundated with statistics that inform us we should expect diseases like cancer to be more commonplace in this twenty-first century. What we need is better education at a far earlier stage. Prevention has to be preferable to trying to find a cure for disease.

We were painfully aware of the serious depth to which Matt had suffered physically as a result of his illness, and especially since much of the damage to his body had gone visibly undetected until it was too late. So far, miraculously he had survived, and his body showed small signs of healthy activity once again. However, we realised that although our shots in the dark had gained some time, what was desperately needed was a regulated plan of nutrition, including the right proteins, bioflavinoids, vitamins, minerals and amino acids, tailor-made for Matt that would assist his body to fight any malignancy he may have and ultimately regain good health.

As a result of the course I had attended we were also beginning to understand something of the body's digestive system and so began giving Matthew special enemas to assist his body in its vital eliminating process. Gentle enemas can be an important aid for the body to rid itself of toxins by opening up the bile ducts and preventing undue strain on the liver. Although it involved a lot more time and effort, this process had a direct influence on the reduction of Matt's vomiting and regularity of his bowel movements and we were encouraged by what we witnessed.

What became apparent was, though Matthew was bed-bound and considerably paralysed, his body was now maintaining a regular pattern of disposal of waste product. The juices, delivered absolutely fresh for optimum benefits, were delivering nutrition into the bloodstream within thirty minutes of being administered, without his body using precious energy to convert that food, so making it quickly available for the body's own healing process.

Because the conventional doctors were unable to offer further treatment for Matt and we had chosen to give him alternative therapy at home, we were limited in monitoring any changes that occurred in his body, other than our powers of observation, although these improved daily. But we were sometimes rewarded with small indications that his condition, far from deteriorating, showed optimistic signs of improvement.

It was tempting to seek tangible proof that the treatments were making a difference, perhaps in the form of a scan, but that would have involved a return to hospital and we still believed it would not be beneficial to Matt at that time. He remained stable and seemed happier at home. We continued to nurse, research and pray as we waited and learned.

Chapter 26

The time we spent together as a family then was very precious. It may seem strange to say, since Matthew had been given a shocking and terminal diagnosis, but we had that time with each other to the exclusion of everyone else if we chose. Progress seemed frustratingly slow and we discovered that patience is not just a virtue but a necessity if we were to stay the course and, almost as a sideline, Mark and I discovered marriage is a meaty subject! We both believed our relationship was something never to be taken for granted, always to be worked at and always worth your best effort, but then there's reality and nothing prepares you for marriage in those circumstances. How often we profess to hold up principles that we subsequently struggle to uphold!

They were painfully honest times for us as a couple as well as a family. Honesty makes you incredibly vulnerable, but it also cuts to the chase. Time is a precious commodity and we were discovering it was not to be wasted nurturing emotional hurts, real or imagined. To experience suffering first-hand heightened our awareness of pain and hammered home the fact that we do not know how long we have on this earth. Because our lives were being played out like some soap opera around Matt's bedside, we were keen to be honest and open with him too about our feelings. We included him in conversations, much more than before his illness, and even though he was unable to physically answer, we developed a kind of code of expressions that spoke volumes.

Our relationship began in 1985 though we did not get married until 1991 when Matt was two. We lived as many busy couples with children do. We socialised with friends and tried to have quality time together but sixteen years down the line, there remained big chunks of who we were deep down, largely unplumbed. Spending twenty-four hours in every day with someone you profess to love is challenging enough but our circumstances put additional strains on us. We were forced to examine our characters, our personalities and some of the things we discovered were not endearing.

I had grown up with the distorted view that people's acceptance of me was based on my performance and so for many years I strove for a perfectionism impossible to attain. I was critical of others who failed to reach those unattainable levels too. It was agonisingly painful for me to allow Mark the freedom to do things in ways he was comfortable with and not get stressed about it.

That was another valuable lesson. Stress is a powerful enemy, capable of destroying relationships and undermining health. We all react differently to stress, affected by our genetic makeup, our background and our environment. We both fell victim to its perils though I discovered stress was potentially more visibly destructive to me than to Mark, and if I did not do something to change, it could have far reaching effects on my life. Piecing together more bits of the jigsaw, we were able to see that anxiety and stress were no strangers to Matthew either.

Initially we had chosen not to tell him exactly what was wrong with him but, in the safety of our home, we shared certain relevant facts with him. Our intention was not to overload him with information, but to reassure him that we loved each other and him very much and would do all that we possibly could to help him. When things got too much and we vented our frustrations on each other, Mark and I tried to forgive each other really quickly to alleviate any bad atmospheres, though looking back it was often difficult to achieve and we definitely weren't as prompt as we could have been in that department.

We were slowly realising that we had survived the most challenging time of our lives. But not through choice. There was no short cut, no way around, no way out, just straight through. There was no time off for good behaviour, no rest until we felt able to continue and no one else to blame or pass our situation on to. We were still on our way up the mountain, fingernail by fingernail, following those small steps forward in Matt's progress. After almost ten months of illness and being confined to bed, his limbs were less active than before and he spent a large part of the day sleeping but, when he was awake and alert, we glimpsed the precious person we knew and loved so well, albeit trapped inside his inactive body.

Mark and I were always notoriously lax at having films developed promptly. This was painfully illustrated when that January we developed a film containing pictures of Matthew a few days before his illness became apparent, together with photos taken at perhaps his lowest ebb in hospital and then snaps taken on his recent birthday. It was hard to look at the chronological collage of our lives and not feel pain at our ignorance of what tomorrow could bring. But, conversely we were encouraged to see his progress. As we fed him foods that were invaluable in the fight against disease, it fed our hope as we waited for that miracle.

We had said all along that we were relying totally on God for Matthew's healing. If He chose to use conventional medicines, that would be fine, alternative treatments, equally fine, an instantaneous miracle, absolutely positively fine. But ultimately we believed only God could heal our son and we had to rely on Him, and that meant trusting His timing too, without checking up on Him. It felt like driving around town with a blindfold on and trusting the instructions and guidance of the person sitting in the seat next to you! Scary!!! Except we kept reminding ourselves, the person next to us was none other than God Himself.

During that February 2002, a lady journalist from the Sunday Times colour supplement spent the best part of a day with us. After seeing an article in our local paper about Matthew's fight with cancer and the alternative treatments he was having, she was interested in presenting a possible series on his progress. Diet, nutrition and supplements are hot property when it comes to fighting disease these days. Apparently people are seeking alternatives to the accepted medical treatments and a number of them have success stories to tell.

It was a challenging day for us as we covered events and feelings since April 27th the previous year. We were especially struck by how many times we felt the need to mention God's part in our lives throughout all of this and we hoped that the article would reflect our faith in a way that people would find easy to understand and not be put off by it. We looked forward to the next stage when a photographer would come and take lots of pictures of Matthew in preparation for the article.

Mark's grandmother died that January and he was able to attend her funeral to reflect on her amazing 100 years of healthy life. Living a near self-sufficient lifestyle, she grew all her own vegetables in her acre of garden, did not own a television, spoke fluent French and kept her shorthand skills up to date. She would willingly have traded some of her latter years for Matt though and was happy to at last be going home. My maternal grandmother, with whom I was especially close, died a few years before, and she too knew her beloved Jesus with an enviable intimacy and thanks to her relentless prayers I finally became a Christian a few years before her death. She lived to see profound changes in me and I hope my progress since will further delight her when we meet again.

Her faith inspired me, and we would spend many hours talking about Jesus and what it would be like when we met Him face to face. She would always say, with a twinkle in her eye, that she would let me know how wonderful He was. Between her death and funeral, my job took me overnight to Turin where I had a dream so vivid, I thought it real for ages after waking. For many months before her death from lung cancer, she had to wear an oxygen mask and as she laboured to breathe her chest rasped painfully. As a toddler Matt always called her 'nanny breathe'.

In my dream, I was awakened from sleep by my nanna calling my name. When I answered she told me to listen to her chest. Her breathing made no laboured sound and she smiled as she said, "He's healed me Lyn, and do you know, He's even more beautiful than we could ever have imagined."

That dream has sustained me enormously over the years and given me such a sense of excitement about eternal life. We've always told Matthew how special he is to Jesus and, since his illness, I know from the look on his face that he drew much comfort from that knowledge. We both look forward to the day when we shall see those two amazing ladies again and to a time when there will no longer be suffering in this world and tears will fall no more. When six month old babies will not have leukaemia and children will no longer die from starvation in a world where mountains of food rot away unused.

So we fought on and looked forward to a world where hate is excluded because people love each other so much. A world where money and power has no meaning or worth.

A world where difficult lessons will not be on the curriculum, pain will no longer be an emotion that torments our souls, and we will behold our Jesus – more beautiful than we could ever imagine.

Chapter 27

At the beginning of March 2002, and following on from an impromptu raffle held at a local supermarket just before Christmas, a new-found friend and ex-nurse Sara, who helped us with Matt's care whenever she could, took on the mammoth task of organising a week-long raffle in our local town. On her own initiative, she contacted many businesses in the area, telling them about Matthew and asking for prize donations.

It was well supported and a stand was set up in the town centre displaying pictures of us all and details of Matt's brave fight against his illness. It was a resounding success and the money raised further financed Matthew's care without the need for either Mark or myself to seek work at a time when it would have been impossible. We are so grateful for acts of love such as this and the sacrificial way people worked and gave to achieve tremendous success.

Simultaneously, friends and members of our previous and current church got together to organise a concert in honour of Matthew at a local school in Windsor. They wanted to do something for him and us to raise some money for his continued care. The commitment given to the preparation of the evening showed such love and devotion to us as a family and was a resounding success. Musicians gathered and performed great music they knew Matt would approve of. Dancers danced and comperes and organisers alike gave their all. Friends, gifted in all things technical, put together a pictorial story of Matt's life and an interview with us all filmed at home that was shown during the evening.

Matthew's school friends joined in with some innovative ventures to help raise money to add to their swelling coffers. Auctions were held for worthy prizes that had been generously donated by businesses and individuals, and raffles and other entrepreneurial ventures were held throughout the evening. The end result was a musical recording for us to treasure and share with Matt at home, an overwhelming donation in excess of £12,000 and memories of boundless love that would never end. Feeling too vulnerable to appear at such an emotional event, I entrusted the privilege to Mark, who bravely attended while I stayed home with a willing friend holding hands with the star of the show.

It was also in that March that we were recommended to contact an organisation called the Nutritional Cancer Therapy Trust founded in 1995 by a retired biochemist. Through a uniquely tailored diet and supplements their holistic objective is to help restore the health of patients suffering from cancer and other degenerative illnesses. Following voluntary work in hospices during his retirement, founder Chris Ashton wanted to offer patients the best choices in alternative treatments. We phoned to arrange a meeting with Chris and were impressed and encouraged by his caring and friendly approach.

A prompt visit followed and the next two weeks were spent in busy preparation for Matthew to begin the specialised diet and nutritional regime. We discovered that much of what we were already giving Matthew was along the right lines. It was essential that everything we fed him was organic, and any water that came into contact with him had to be as free from chemicals and additives as possible to assist his body in a detoxification and healing process.

Although in the United Kingdom we can turn on our indoor taps and have access to drinking water, that water is not as harmless as we may think and in many areas contains so many noxious substances as to be threatening to certain people whose constitutions are weakened by disease.

All the generous financial donations made it possible for us to install a simple device under our kitchen sink that filtered virtually all impurities from the water whilst leaving essential minerals in – a process called reverse osmosis. This was the only water that Matt should come into contact with either for drinking, mixing with medicines or treatments, washing vegetables and last and definitely least in Matt's opinion, washing him! The aim of the treatment was to detoxify his body of anything that was harmful to him, and assist in building up his immune system thereby enabling his body to repair damage done by disease, chemical treatments and chemical medications and ultimately to bring his body to a state of health that would sustain life in the long term.

The Trust itself does not make any charges to patients, relying solely on sponsors, but nutrients and supplements have to be purchased by the patient and there are some charges made by attending consultants. One thing I will say is that the Trust outline absolutely everything at the outset, so that the patient or their family can ascertain whether it is financially feasible for them to proceed and whether they are able to undergo the rigorous regime. Taking into account all the various treatments, supplements and nutrients that we had tried for Matthew already, we did not feel that the overall cost was excessively high, and anyway, this was our son and I know both Mark and I were prepared to do whatever it took to give Matt the best possible chance of survival. Thankfully the donated funds continued like the widow's oil.

An air of excitement hung over us as we ticked off the days to Treatment Day One. Our invaluable juicer would continue to earn its keep, supplying a constant flow of the freshest juices, all made from organic vegetables and fruits. Changing lifelong habits almost overnight, we threw out existing washing powders, soaps, toothpaste and a whole list of no-nos that were counterproductive to the treatment because of their chemical ingredients. Concurrent with all this, the Trust recommends and prescribes the use of homeopathic medicines to assist in the body's natural healing process.

This latter aspect was quite a big step for us, as we had always dismissed homeopathy as being ineffectual, considering it a mind over matter approach due to the way it was prepared. It is totally different to conventional allopathic medicine, which uses drugs having the opposite effects to the symptoms. Homeopathy considers the whole person and uses minute doses of substances that have been proven to produce symptoms of the illness in a healthy individual. The aim is to stimulate the body's own defence mechanism to address the underlying cause of illness. Homeopathy enjoys huge patronage and success in all walks of life but, erroneously, it is not always given the attention it deserves. The more I study the intricate workings of the human body and its Creator, the more I am convinced that it is a valuable form of alternative treatment.

From our faith point of view it was also challenging as we had always upheld opinions that viewed homeopathy in an unattractive light. But after careful consideration, prayer and counsel from respected friends and professional people, much patient explanation from Chris Ashton and more research on the internet, we had to admit that our views had been formulated on scant knowledge, some misinformation and misunderstanding – and we finally decided to try it for Matthew.

With hindsight, we both believe that we would have preferred to adopt the recommendations of the Trust, whilst maintaining certain other treatments that we believe were having a beneficial effect on Matt, but at the time we chose to continue with their preferred methods only. It is our conviction now that in any complex illness such as cancer, because the causes are likely to be multiple, so also is the cure and we should keep a very open mind to all treatments that are available.

As we entered the ninth month since coming home, we more fully appreciated the magnitude of our endeavour. I'm totally persuaded that neither of us had any real concept of what this undertaking might entail at the outset. Whilst convinced that our love for our son would encourage us to do the same again, with hindsight, I'm not sure our courage would stand the test to make such a long-term commitment at the outset. It was a daunting feeling to be responsible for everything for Matthew. As I have expressed before, there were countless times when we felt so alone, so exhausted. Our knowledge was growing but compared to Matthew's serious condition it was sadly limited. To have the Trust working alongside us, totally dedicated to helping Matthew and always available at the end of the telephone to answer our constant questions, was almost overwhelming in its comfort.

Chapter 28

As March 2002 tempted us with brief glimpses of Spring, a few weeks of stability and progress tempted us with further hope as our son outlived the doctors' prognosis by more than six months. With additional invaluable weekly input from the private physiotherapist, Mark was better able to keep up with the daily exercises on Matt's limbs. Everyone's efforts were rewarded one afternoon as three of us managed to slowly sit him up in bed and gently swing his legs around onto the floor. It was a delicate operation, as we had to support his head, back and limbs throughout and not lift him too quickly as he had been lying down for almost eleven months!

I was positioned in front of Mattie, holding his legs and feet, and was privileged to witness the most amazing wide-eyed expression and noticeable intake of breath as he looked out of our patio doors from a vertical position for the first time in almost a year. It was such a precious gift and tears filled my eyes. Our boy child was now every inch a young man, so tall, so changed, so handsome. I wanted to scoop him into my arms and hug him but I didn't have a spare arm. He even slowly, falteringly raised his right arm and seemed to point shakily forward. There followed no adverse side-effects; it was an understatement to say we were delirious with joy.

Unable yet to communicate much verbally to us, we did not know what our son was thinking or how he felt, or even most times whether he experienced any pain. Just by studying his expressive eyes we could sense life burning strongly within him and the will and strength to tackle each day with us. We continued with his new feeding regime adjusting and fine-tuning his intake of necessary supplements as well as continuing with aloe vera, flax seed oil and some valuable proteins in the way of organic round brown rice and red lentils. These were still given to him by the only means available to us, via the naso-gastric tube down his nose and throat and into his stomach.

The tube was in itself a mixed blessing because, as essential as it was, it was tiny and extremely prone to blocking if we hadn't liquidised food and medicines enough. That meant a lengthy delay as we had to extract it and insert a new one which was an unpleasant task as it easily caused Matt to gag and retch during insertion. Mark was brilliant as he had learned how to do it himself but, even so, it was an event I came to dread, and so I believe did Matt.

Many of the things we gave Matthew and subjected him to we tested on ourselves first, so that we could know something of what he was experiencing. Mark bravely allowed me an attempt at inserting a tube down his nose and throat, but interestingly neither he nor I could complete the task as he was retching so much and I was too anxious – all of which caused me to respect and admire Matthew and Mark so much more.

With hindsight we probably would have requested that a feeding tube was inserted directly into Matthew's stomach while he was still in hospital, but it was never offered in those early days as his diagnosis was initially unknown and, when it was, the doctors were not expecting Matt to live very long. We both believe that a different means of feeding Matthew would have made things infinitely easier for us as his carers and immeasurably more comfortable for him, as the tube also seemed to frequently aggravate the congestion of phlegm in his throat.

It is truly amazing to discover what we are capable of when the chips are down. A favourite story of mine is told by Corrie ten Boom who, with her family, hid Jews from the Nazis in occupied Holland during the Second World War. They lived constantly with the knowledge that they may be caught and punished. When she voiced fears of being tortured, her father offered comfort by reminding her that as a young girl on weekly train visits to Amsterdam, he only gave her the train ticket as she was about to board the train, just when she needed it. This illustrates that God gives us grace to deal with each situation in our lives just when we need it, not before, not after, but at exactly the right time. I truly believe all three of us were only able to cope with those nightmare events because we were given grace at precisely the right moment.

A girlfriend with a degree in geology, affectionately referred to by me as a rockologist, gave us a beautiful gift of a glass heart before Matt became ill. It has exquisite purple and turquoise colours swirling inside and is shot through with what appear to be fractures in the glass. I am assured it is a Chinese fluorite. Matt and I have always loved looking at it, especially against the backdrop of the sun, when the fractures intensify and highlight the colours, giving the shape added interest, beauty and depth.

I used to get myself into a bit of a lather every month, as I prepared to send regular updates to everyone praying for us but often couldn't think of anything clever to say, as my mind seemed blank! God said: "Don't be clever Lynette, just be real"! He showed me 'real' one day whilst looking at our glass heart. As events panned out that year, my heart felt like it had been broken – not just once, but fractured over and over and over again.

I spoke to God at length about it, asking Him how I could possibly be of any use to anyone anymore with such a broken, fractured heart. All the pain I felt rendered me practically helpless. "Ah, but there you are," God replied, "that's exactly how you can be of use to anyone. Until you have been through your brokenness, you will be unable to help anyone else go through theirs. Compassionate head knowledge is all very well, but until you have experienced pain and suffering to the point where you can live with it as your companion, you cannot fully empathise with others and help them through their suffering. And anyway, I like broken," He said. "I like things that are broken and then put back together again. They have an exquisite, real beauty."

I suddenly saw clearly, possibly for the first time in my life, that I often confused beauty with symmetry and perfection. If something was untarnished, unbroken and unblemished, I could appreciate its beauty. God was showing me beauty in everything, especially the broken, the damaged, the hurting, the things that do not conform to our world's view of acceptable. I was learning how broken people who have experienced suffering are the very ones qualified to reach out to a needy world.

At school, if I made a mistake in an exercise book I would hurriedly tear out that page and begin my work again so that it would show no evidence of my mistakes. But God's simple truth is, it is our experiences and mistakes, and the very signs of brokenness, fractures and wear and tear that give us our depth, our character, our interest, our usefulness and our beauty.

I began to realise Mark, in his brokenness, saw himself as a husband and father who had failed, whose life had been turned upside down, who in faith did the best he could though feeling sadly inadequate. But Matt and I experienced a passionately caring man who didn't get everything right, but who was always there for us, and who would willingly take all our hurts and pains upon himself. A man who lovingly read the Bible to us every day to encourage and strengthen us.

I saw Matt, presently unable to speak or move by himself, whose life had been fractured and broken, yet hundreds of people around the world saw faith and strength in him and were inspired. We experienced a maturing young man who silently and courageously endured an excess of life's greatest hardships at a tender age.

I saw myself as a mother whose heart had been so fractured by the devastating pain of my child's illness that I feared I would never function normally again, yet who was learning to empathise with suffering because I had experienced it first hand. And God saw all three of us and said, "My precious children, you are so beautiful to me, let me use you to show others how beautiful they are."

Chapter 29

As soon as his new treatment began Matthew was prescribed homeopathic remedies for the troublesome phlegm. They took some adjusting as initially they over-stimulated the process and produced more, but we eventually witnessed an improvement in him. Mark, backed by both physiotherapists, was amazed to detect tangible movement, this time in Matt's left hand. Twice he was able to raise it slightly and move it unaided across the bed towards his body. It would be an understatement to say we felt excited.

It was through the Nutritional Cancer Therapy Trust that another lovely young lady came into Matt's life. He was accumulating quite a fan club. Sally Hawkins initially oversaw all his homeopathic treatment but soon became a friend. As well as working as a consultant for the Trust, she was a homeopathic doctor in her own right and fortuitously lived only five minutes away by car. We know that because we ran her through her paces at ten o'clock one evening, shortly after meeting her, when Matt suffered a series of small seizures.

Due to the gravity of Matthew's condition, he was by no means textbook stuff; so much of his homeopathic treatment was learned and adjusted on the hoof as it were. Matt was charting new territory in more ways than one. An incredible breakthrough for us was that remedies given to him for the seizures most definitely had an immediate and beneficial effect. This was especially encouraging as it occurred simultaneously as we reduced his chemical medication for their control. Because many chemical drugs often produce undesirable side-effects you cannot always discontinue them instantly, but must do so over a protracted and monitored period of time. As the drugs registered less and less in his blood tests, the seizures which had been erratic, frightening and draining, far from worsening were of shorter duration and less debilitating for Matt.

One huge difference these small but important changes made for Mark and me was the freedom for one of us to occasionally be occupied somewhere else in the house, or even venture out to collect our weekly order of organic vegetables without arranging additional care cover. We were permanently attached to a mobile phone throughout but the sense of relief that these short expeditions gave us fortified us enormously to return home and carry on with renewed vigour. After our prolonged incarceration, the world seemed a noisy aggressive place and we were always pleased to return to the peace and calm of our living room. We hoped that our own change of environment brought a promise of freedom to Matthew too as he lay imprisoned in his bed. He always seemed pleased to see each of us return. Our small steps of progress helped us nurture dreams of new horizons for us all.

Mark continued relentlessly every day with the ever-lengthening physio exercises. I'm not so sure Matthew was always delighted at his tenacity but I was, knowing I should not have the same determination to put Matt through his necessary paces when sometimes it clearly caused him discomfort. It was becoming more apparent that each of us possessed gifts and abilities we could use to help our son and we were ever thankful to be a partnership in the monumental task.

Matthew's special bed was living up to its expectations as remarkably he suffered no bed sores in all the time he was bed bound. Like children, both Mark and I scrambled to try out the bed whenever Matthew was safely ensconced in the wheelchair. Mark did a good impersonation of Goldilocks on it one day, misnomer though that may be, but you get my drift! Long-term sleep deprivation rendered us capable of nodding off anywhere!

Under the pretext of studying and keeping Matt company I fell asleep on the sofa one afternoon, with my mouth wide open and a book slumped on my face, only to awaken to the shrill sound of our front doorbell. I called Mark but receiving no answer from him sleepily answered the door and showed the physiotherapist into the lounge. Mark suddenly appeared from down by the side of Matt's bed where he had fallen asleep on the floor. It's not easy, pretending you have been making some minor adjustment under the bed, when you have carpet imprint all up one side of your face!

At about the same time Michelle the trainee nurse regretably informed us that she would no longer be able to help due to urgent course work. Quite independently, our lovely Marie Curie nurses got together and arranged for one of them to give assistance for four hours of day care biweekly. What we lost on the swings, we gained more or less on the roundabouts and so were able to continue with our taxing schedule.

Several invitingly warm days in May that year encouraged us to venture out into the garden with Matt in his wheelchair covered with his favourite leopard blanket. It was difficult to know from his limited facial expressions whether he was happy doing so or not, but we assumed he was comfortable with small degrees of change and complied with any obvious signs of discomfort by returning him promptly to the familiarity of his bed.

Mark and I prayed daily for Matthew to be able to communicate his desires to us; we longed for a breakthrough in that area. Underneath it all was a teenage boy who had suffered heartbreaking trauma over the past twelve months and who undoubtedly felt trapped inside his inactive body. Although he had heard many things about his illness, he was unable to express his feelings or ask questions. He had to spend twenty-four hours a day with his parents, relying on them and trusting them for everything. We had to trust that Matt's spirit and emotions would experience the same miraculous healing we desired for his physical body.

That first year we felt surrounded by a furious storm of freak proportions in our ordinary lives. And yet, there were countless times when we experienced a peace and stillness around us that was beyond our understanding. A friend remarked in the early days of Matt's illness that sometimes the safest place to be in a storm was in the very centre – in the eye. Mayhem swirled around and about us for months and yet in the very centre, right where we were, we often felt calm, buoyant and sustained. I prayed our precious boy felt that peace too.

Of course, our faith was strengthened by knowing so many people were willing us on, praying for us, caring for us and loving us during those times. It was often only the faith of others that sustained us in the darkest days and nights, the love people expressed to us in so many different ways that made it possible for us to survive when we could no longer see a way to carry on. Reality is that the sun rises and sets on us all in the same way. Bad things do happen to ordinary people. There are no pat answers, no clever solutions, but God is God, no matter what and in Him we choose to put our trust. I heard one day that when the storms of life come, they do so on all houses, but it's our foundations that are crucial; they will determine whether we will sink into the sand or stand firm on the rock. That Rock for Mark, Mattie and me was Jesus. There were no substitutes, He was the real thing.

Chapter 30

On July 10th 2002, I wrote in my journal: *"For fifteen months it seems we have been living in a long dark tunnel. I can't recall the worst point because there have been many. Sometimes we couldn't see any light from the beginning nor light at the end."*

That may sound odd, having so strongly professed our faith, but we discovered that you can still believe in God with all your heart, soul, mind and strength – know that He is with you every step you take – and yet feel totally surrounded by a dark tunnel and experience times when you can't hear His voice at all. But we trusted God was there, because He had promised to be, even though we couldn't always feel His presence. Just as the sun was assuredly in the sky, even when hidden from our sight by thick clouds, He was there. Even if we never understood why this had happened to us, He was there.

Day after day we continued to believe and trust Him – that He had our best interests at heart, no matter what the outcome. Sometimes we cried out in sheer desperation or frustration. I did a lot of banging around in the tunnel, hitting the walls and characteristically making a lot of noise instead of waiting quietly and patiently. But the bruises I sustained have helped me to better understand myself a lot more and deal with some issues that have been with me for a long time. Mark doesn't display so many bruises – not noticeably anyway – and he has been an inspiration to me and I hope to Matt. His unwavering faith and calmness in dire circumstances gave this family an anchor and lifeline. Many times, I silently watched him ponder a hopeless situation, square his shoulders, take a deep breath and say: "Don't worry, it's going to be all right. We are going to get through this." In the presence of such determination and courage, I could only throw in my lot with the bookies' rank outsider against a daunting Goliath.

As we celebrated thirteen months since bringing Matt home from hospital and four months since he began his treatment with the Nutritional Cancer Therapy Trust, I can only reiterate how wonderfully supportive that organisation was. They made no false or unrealistic promises, but gave us practical organised tasks and helped us focus on realistic goals whilst never making us feel as if our situation was already a hopeless case with a foregone conclusion. They did not buffer us with false hope, but rather offered sensitive encouragement.

They advised, assisted, answered endless questions and remained on call for us at all times, including bank holidays! We are extremely grateful not only for their professional service but their genuine love. The special diet and nutritional support specifically tailored for Matt seemed to be agreeing with him and was hopefully helping his body fight this dreadful disease. He was getting stronger by the week. That was apparent by the renewed finger-pointing and waving of his right hand and arm.

Something we found common amongst all the consultants we dealt with concerning alternative remedies, was a strong personal commitment to the patient. We always felt that Matthew was given undivided attention, something that is not always possible in a busy and overcrowded national health system. In contrast to the approach of the conventional medical profession, these people, all specialists in their fields, were prepared to listen to the opinions and observations of Mark and me and in fact insisted upon it as they made their appraisals of Matt's situation and planned any further treatment. It greatly encouraged us that they took so much notice of what we had to say and comforting to think that they were making decisions greatly influenced by our observational input.

With hindsight we both regret not seeking a second opinion within the conventional medical system at the very outset of Matt's illness. We both now believe we should have postponed the chemotherapy and certainly the biopsy, which left him so disabled, while we investigated all possible alternative treatments at that strategic point in his illness before committing our son to painful and possibly damaging, irreversible treatment.

Matthew's regime began at about eight-thirty in the morning with freshly squeezed grapefruit and lemon juice, finding the optional orange juice a little acidic for him. Immediately following were his first supplements of the day, a large dose of powdered Vitamin C, with liquid aloe vera and exacting amounts of special formula tablets containing specially balanced vitamins, minerals, amino acids and other ingredients geared to boost his immune system. All of the tablets had to be split open, as they are manufactured in capsule form, and then liquified with enough water to be able to administer them via the extremely narrow tube from his nose, to his stomach. Any water used had to be the specially filtered water provided by the reverse osmosis apparatus.

Breakfast about nine o'clock was carefully measured amounts of millet, to provide a good source of easily-absorbed protein, in flaked form soaked overnight and then made into a porridge fresh each morning, adding water to further liquify. That was followed by more supplements. Around ten was another juice, this time carrot with apple, specifically the sharp, hard green ones, which yield maximum benefits. All the juices were freshly prepared, using organic fruits and vegetables and organic grains and pulses were compulsory, to reduce the possibility of any chemicals or toxic substances used in their production. Elevenses was yet another juice, often beetroot and carrot.

Throughout the therapy, Mark and I more than once subjected ourselves to exist purely on what Matthew was having. It was interesting to note that within a very short time of drinking the juices, even when we had eaten nothing else, we felt both energised and satisfied. Lunch was preceded by more of the specifically balanced supplements accompanied by short grain organic brown rice, turmeric and garlic. The brown rice proved to be the bane of our lives because no matter how much water it was cooked in and mixed with, it was seldom liquid enough to pass down the tube without a great deal of effort, often causing a blockage and requiring the tube to be changed – a frustrating and uncomfortable operation for everyone concerned.

Both of us had calluses appearing on our palms where we were continuously administering Matt's food and medicines from a plastic syringe down through the tube but Mark, who was frequently called upon to despatch the troublesome brown rice, had numerous blisters, sores and scars that never had time to heal before the next onslaught. Even now, I can vividly picture the deep cuts down the sides of his fingers and thumbs from continuously pushing the syringes and frequently washing the juicing equipment.

All the time, Mattie would watch us with his expressive eyes, and I don't ever remember him conveying fear, pain or displeasure. I always joked with him when serving him fresh beetroot juice as beetroot was something he previously would not be seen in the same room with let alone allowing it to be put into his body! He would indulgently look me straight in the eye and perhaps raise one eyebrow. Witnessing his courage and fortitude gave us the strength and inspiration to endure each arduous day.

His mid-afternoon juice cocktail would consist of vegetables, including green pepper, red cabbage, watercress, cos lettuce, a little cauliflower or broccoli, some parsley and garlic often mixed with green apple, followed down with potassium supplement in liquid form. We did not have to give him any additional water as he was receiving sufficient from the fresh juices and that mixed with his solids and supplements.

Dinner was à la carte and our choice – either the rice mix again or red lentils preceded and followed by more supplements, aloe vera and vitamin C and one final juice was given mid-evening. Red lentils were certainly a popular choice come evening time, as by then we were exhausted and our hands were crying out in pain. All in all it was an exhausting schedule for us to keep on top of and a great deal for Matt to absorb, but that is exactly what his body did and the beneficial results were increasingly visible. His skin was beautiful, blemish free and glowing and his eyes were alert and clear. His hair shone and grew rapidly and his nails were healthy and strong and needed regular cutting as they too grew quickly.

During a check-up visit from the Cancer Therapy Trust, we were delighted to hear how both Chris and Sally were impressed by Matt's progress and encouraged by his healthy appearance. My son, who always looked gorgeous before, was strikingly handsome now and I make no excuses for being biased.

One interesting and heartening development was that Matthew suffered quite badly from hay fever again that year. He had shown no signs of it at all the previous year. We thought perhaps the anti seizure medication had been sedating him so much he wasn't affected, but Sally said that cancer patients seldom suffer from hay fever and other allergies when they are very ill, as their immune system is so run down it is unable to react to outside stimuli. That he was once more affected, albeit an uncomfortable inconvenience to Matt, indicated that his immune system was kicking in. He was prescribed natural treatment for the hay fever which did the trick, but all the implications were worthy of a celebration or three!

The rest of our daily schedule included washing and changing Matt and then Mark undertook his daily physio while I would perform essential household tasks. For the remaining time in the day, we read to him, listened to music, watched some TV with him, and chatted and played games with him.

Mark writes:
Amidst all the things we needed to do for Matt, I would always push to find time to read to him. I felt it was important both for me and him and what wonderful times they were. It could be during the day or at bedtime, as was our practice before he became ill when it had been our special time together. Then we would both squeeze onto his single bed or dangle precariously on top of his bunk, just reading and chatting, father and son. I clung fiercely to that privilege even as he grew older. Life just stopped when we shared those times and the feeling of intimacy was incredible.

I have never been much of a reader. Lynette, herself a bookworm, always joked that before we met I had only read one book and that was Frank Bruno's autobiography, so no great literary challenge. Forgive me Frank, but "Know what I mean?" But with Matt it was always different. He just loved stories, factual or fictional and much preferred someone reading them to him than as a solitary pastime. Obviously his father's son.

At least once a day I would pull my stool up close to his bed as we shut out the rest of the world. Lynette would usually leave us alone to do necessary chores around the house and for a while we were transported back to those seemingly distant times that were just precious memories. I read anything I could lay my hands on – mostly Christian books, but not 'namby-pamby' stuff. I knew Matt liked stories of people living on the edge, being challenged and performing amazing feats or really entertaining tales told with a wacky humour that matched his own.

It seems odd to say but I really enjoyed that time we spent imprisoned in our lounge, with all the worries of the outside world a million miles away and only the distant sounds of children in our lane on their way to and from school. As we read about heaven and hell, martyrs and heroes who died for their faith and kids who made a difference in this madcap world, I wondered if my boy would ever be on his way home from school again. I hoped he would with all my heart. God spoke to me a lot during those times; I pray that He spoke to Mattie too reassuring him and telling him how special he was.

Chapter 31

The icing on the cake that July was Matthew's amazing efforts to speak to us. Initially only a few clear simple words, but he continually tried to vocalise his thoughts. One such incident occurred when Mark and I were changing him and I asked him a question but characteristically chatted on without waiting for an answer. A few moments later, a tentative little voice answered, "Yeeees." A comical picture I'm certain – two adults jumping up and down dancing, if you can call it that, and punching the air victoriously. Other similar incidents happened more and more frequently and it became clear he was directly answering specific questions – with a simple yes or no – but answering nonetheless.

We usually played music for Matt while preparing to settle him down for the first shift of the night. One evening, Mark had put on a CD and had just disappeared upstairs to change for bed. Matt was on his side, looking really peaceful as I came into the lounge. I said to him, "Oh, you're listening to your 'Blue' CD are you, that's nice" Immediately Matt said softly, "Er, yes." I nearly fell over with shock and shouted upstairs to share my excitement with Mark. As well as being a really prompt answer, more pertinently, it was exactly relevant. That particular CD was one we bought Matt for Christmas after the onset of his illness. Not only did he answer the question, but he knew, post illness, who the band were and that the CD was his, illustrating that his cognitive thought process was working.

One Sunday Mark attended church for the evening service leaving me on duty and Matt and I were half listening to a pop music party in Hyde Park on the television. I was sitting next to the bed, holding his hand as I often did when the chores were done; it was always a precious time. I looked into his eyes and said, "I love you Mattie" He looked intently at me and opening his mouth, moved his tongue to the roof of his mouth and I'm sure, tried his hardest to form the word 'love'. Trust me, I know, I'm his mother. That was "Love you too, infinity and beyond!"

My eyes filled with tears as I realised we were listening to a song called 'Flying Without Wings'. The words are all about finding a certain something in life that makes you feel as if you are flying without wings. For the first time in many hearings of that song, I understood what it could feel like – to fly without wings. My son, whose voice I had barely heard for almost a year, was trying with all his strength to tell me that he loved me, in our secret way. I was up there – high up there, with the eagles. Above the storm.

During that July I attended the funeral and memorial service for our ex-Pastor's wife following a long, brave battle with cancer. In spite of eighteen months of living with the threat of death, she had no fear of it, because her faith assured her of an eternal life to look forward to. She trusted God no matter what. During her illness her faith inspired us to hang on and then hang on some more. Someone said the day was a mixture of the bitter and sweet. It was. As friends and family expressed sadness at her premature departure from this world, they could not but feel an overflowing of joy because she was with the Jesus she so loved and, for her at least, the labour of this life was over.

We sang some rousing songs that were food to the soul and listened to her husband, children and friends give worthy tributes. One of her favourite songs was 'Flying Without Wings' and as she was carried from the church the words reminded me again of that special time with my son the day before and more importantly, that our Father in Heaven knows all things we cherish in our hearts, and He alone will carry us through *all* the storms of life.

That early summer was truly a time of blessed hope for our family. Matthew's left arm and leg were progressively showing signs of improved movement. Both his head and his neck were becoming stronger and he was beginning to lift his head off the pillow by himself. It was almost as if he wanted to sit up or get up, or both! He was regularly sitting in his wheelchair in other rooms in the house with us or even outside, weather permitting.

Apart from two slight manifestations, Matthew was virtually seizure-free for over four weeks. We always dreaded the seizures, imagining some sinister reason for them. But Chris Ashton believed their occasional appearance now was more likely to be signs of the body healing and ridding itself of toxins from the illness and residue of the blood clot sustained during the biopsy, that the treatment should be breaking down. We learned not to fear them, but to pray with Matt when they occurred, reassuring him and helping him through them.

I kept threatening to do some serious walking for an hour a day and Mark wanted to start running again or at least some form of exercise. But it was too exciting just being together and we didn't like missing anything. So good intentions were shelved, although Mark and I were individually able to enjoy outings that month – an encouraging sign as it reflected a slight ease in our own tenseness.

I was treated to theatre tickets that July to see Riverdance 2002 in London, which was one of Matt's and my favourites. Clutching the programme on my return I gave him a detailed verbal account of the action but restrained myself from actual physical demonstrations, though I do a rather good impersonation of a wooden peg dancing. The second treat was to see a comedy performed in a beautiful mill setting at a local Berkshire theatre. Both provided wonderful entertainment and more importantly helped me to relax and think about things outside our living room. We both managed to attend some of our church meetings and forever young, in his mind at least, Mark attended a local pop concert with friends. But we still chose that one of us should always be with Matthew – partly because his treatment schedule was complicated and frequently being 'tweaked' but partly because we believed he still required that continuity. We certainly did.

Our night times had changed somewhat too. Instead of two-or four-hourly shifts of sleeping and keeping watch, the invaluable help of our Marie Curie nurses three nights a week meant that only one of us needed to remain in the lounge and the other one could enjoy a luxury night for one upstairs in a proper bed! We came to love Olivia, Rhiannon and Heather enormously, but we both eagerly welcomed our turn to disappear upstairs. I would frequently wake up in the middle of the night in a complete sweat trying to figure out where on earth Matt's bed was and how to get to the loo! Mark would often try to make the most of his time off by watching a video upstairs but inevitably fell sound asleep long before the end, leaving the film still running and lights blazing!

Chapter 32

At the beginning of August and more than thirteen months after coming home, our lives were inextricably changed once again. As I mentioned, Matthew's school and class mates were extremely supportive from the onset of his illness. As well as keeping us amply provided with wonderful cards and artistic contributions, they had relentlessly beavered away to raise funds to contribute to his treatments. Month after month and event after event they performed their labour of love through cake sales, badge making, car washing and a host of other innovative ideas to help their friend get well. All this was under the guidance of Matt's form teacher, Fiona Smith, or 'Smiffy' as Matt and I affectionately called her.

Mark was asked to attend Trevelyan Middle School in Windsor that July for their final assembly before the summer holidays and the parting of the ways. All the young people in Matthew's year would be moving on to their senior schools. It was an emotional time especially as Mark was presented with a cheque for the monies they had raised. It was a staggering thirteen hundred pounds!

The donated money could easily have been swallowed up in organic carrots, vitamins, lentils, special soaps and extra physiotherapy – amongst other things. But Mark and I remembered a promise, made by a doting father to a very sick son in hospital one day, that went something like this:

"When you are better Matt, you can have a puppy."

Matthew raised an eyebrow.

"In fact, you can have two puppies."

Matthew raised two eyebrows.

Matthew's mother nearly fainted with shock on the other side of the hospital bed! Now we felt Matthew had kept his part of the deal it was time for us to keep ours. So a loving and generous gift from precious school friends was converted into two nine-week-old labrador puppies, who came to live with us.

Madness, I hear you mutter – absolutely! Hard work, I hear you shout – totally! Joy? Did anyone say joy? Well, that's what it meant to us then and particularly to a courageous and brave young thirteen-year-old who could speak volumes with his eyebrows and meant the world to his parents.

Whether later we would thank Trevelyan School, especially Form 8FS and teacher Smiffy, would be debatable. But that August the dogs were a delightful, though very mischievous addition to our family. Inexplicably when they were around Matthew they became gentle and sensitive beyond the knowledge of their short lives. They brought a rather offbeat sense of normality into an otherwise surreal situation.

As for names for those innocent-looking darlings, the adorable chocolate brown bundle was named Samson as his sire was big and strong and we thought his offspring could probably bring the house down – albeit by chewing! The yellow lab, strongly resembling the cute lion cub in 'Lion King', complete with a very crinkly forehead, we called Simba. I remarked to Matt one day that perhaps he didn't like that name, and maybe it was a bit silly, to which he replied, "Nnno, I do." So Simba it was, written in stone!

My memories of that summer will always be accompanied by visions of Mark's attempts at toilet training the puppies. Samson was by far the smarter chap.

Once was enough for him to have his nose thrust all too close to a geographically misplaced package. By day two, he was the world's best-behaved puppy obliging us with obedient toilet rituals and casting condescending glances in Simba's direction.

Not so with old wrinkly brow. I was forever witnessing him being carried to their special area, with a sermon being preached in his ear. I am unsure who cracked first, but Matt, Samson and I were endlessly entertained. Simba was, and still is, an amiable people kind of dog with a selectively short memory – unlike Mark. It was a nail-biting battle of wills. For much of the day the puppies would lie in wait like trained assassins to ambush each other and us with ear-piercing squeals and try out their extremely sharp teeth on yielding flesh.

Matthew was having a spell in his wheelchair most days, often for an hour or longer. We were able to cut his hair successfully whilst he was out of bed and upright. I could only do one look with the clippers but our son was handsome enough to withstand my amateur efforts, unlike his dad who had to call in a professional for a total makeover after my Edward Scissorhands! Matt's eyes looked as big as saucers with his new short haircut – but I liked it. I think we were both amazed at how much he had changed. He was growing up. He looked every bit the teenager he now was.

I think physiotherapy was still a workout that Matthew would rather skip, but considering he had been in bed for more than a year, his body was in good shape and his skin in beautiful condition. Both visiting physiotherapists stretched his capability, which often prompted him to feign sleep when they arrived, but he had now sat on both sides of his bed, with our assistance, and sustained that position for more than five minutes each time without any seeming discomfort. His body was looking very lean, but that can be characteristic on the specialised treatment. They are fed the essential minimum of necessities to fight the illness and fuel the body, whilst not feeding any rogue cells.

The steady improvements in Matthew were quite remarkable to observe especially since it was so long since he had done anything considered normal. When he tried to speak you could tell he was concentrating hard to put his thoughts into sentences. He was not always rewarded for his efforts, but we considered it was progress. We were so thankful for brief glimpses of the young man we lovingly held in our memories and ached to hold in our arms again.

It was good when visitors came, as they were able to put Matt's recovery into perspective. They could see the noticeable changes. It is often our friends who tell us how much our children have grown as our own close proximity prevents our awareness of their changes. The Marie Curie nurses were also noticing minute differences whilst watching Matt at night. They often had to put both legs back into the bed during their shift and closely observed his deft hand movements as he tried to remove the feeding tube in the dark!

Our hope was that the puppies would inspire Matt to move and speak more and motivate him to greater things, preferably before they drove Mark and me to distraction. I became sorely fed up with hearing myself say "No, stop that!" or "No, leave that wire alone." But the two fast-growing perpetrators seemed untroubled by our admonitions and, as I said, afforded us a glimpse of the ordinary in an otherwise extraordinary environment.

Sharing shifts, Mark and I managed to complete the painting of our seemingly endless back garden fence, transforming it into an uplifting shade of blue and our tatty old garden shed was metamorphosed into a willow green.

I hope everyone was as thrilled as we were. Our neighbours were overly gracious about the drips that seeped through during painting but with our lovely blue and white awning, the garden was quite a picture – upturned flowerpots, stolen slippers, chewy bones, sticks and other puppy debris notwithstanding. It all made for more cheerful surroundings whenever the British weather allowed us to venture outside.

We seemed blessed once more during those summer weeks all together, just enjoying each other's company. It was very special to be able to take Matt outside in his wheelchair. One particularly hot afternoon we even went to the trouble of wheeling ninety per cent of his bed through the double patio doors, just so that he could feel the warm breeze on his skin as we all sat under the shady awning. Family, friends and complete strangers continued to lavish care on us. Mark and I were very humbled by people's generosity. Neither of us had worked for well over a year and yet we still had a home, our son had all the essential things he needed to assist his body's healing process and we never suffered a shortage of necessities.

We kept the laptop by Matt's bedside and read e-mails to him of news, jokes and puppy-training advice and our collection of smiley faces on our wall maps grew each week. I secretly nursed a burning desire to write a book about our journey. But our time was still totally occupied with caring for Matthew and his special needs. We put everything else on the back boiler and just basked in the presence of our darling boy.

Chapter 33

A couple of months after we brought Matt home from hospital, I was reading a booklet that accompanied our brilliant juicing machine. It was written by the machine's inventor, an American gentleman who, having cured himself of a serious illness in France drinking only fresh carrot juice, subsequently lived to an exceedingly ripe old age. I was impressed and especially inspired by a particular suggestion he made about living the natural life and, if fortunate enough, acquiring about four-and-a-half acres of land, growing your own vegetables, keeping chickens for eggs, goats for milk and basically leaving the rat race behind.

I began earnestly asking God if we could have some land and grow organic vegetables for Matt and get him fit and strong. My prayers got bolder and I even asked if we could extend some hospitality to other families who had children with cancer and were in a similar situation to ours. Mark joined me in these prayers and we nurtured our little dream of a Promised Land.

After briefly considering Wales in the United Kingdom where it is occasionally still possible to buy land at less than silly prices, our research on the internet led us to several potential sites in France. From experience during holidays, we particularly liked the look of the West coast, bordering the Atlantic ocean, south of La Rochelle, as the climate there is very agreeable with lots of sunshine. We even checked with some old friends about churches in the area and were pleased when we received some good reports back.

I requested copious details from various agents and sat back expectantly awaiting the mail. We have always loved looking at house details. Disappointingly only one agent sent photos and information immediately and, whilst considering our initial requirements, suggested that one place may well fit the bill. We were looking for somewhere that would be immediately habitable, with some other buildings to renovate, a swimming pool for Matt, not too far from the sea and with some land. About four-and-a-half acres would be good!

In the absence of other potential possibilities, we began corresponding about this suggested property with a view to Mark visiting France for forty-eight hours for a whistle-stop tour. The agent was inordinately helpful and although happy for Mark to visit other properties, was inexplicably keen on us seeing one particular property as, in his words, he thought it would "suit our needs perfectly". He explained he would be happy to sell us any property, but preferred to sell what he believed was the right property to the right clients.

Responding to an e-mail in which he said he was looking forward to meeting us both, I told him about Matthew and why it would be impossible for both of us to travel at the same time. He replied, affirming that the property was, in his opinion, even more suitable considering our situation and unique requirements and couldn't wait for us to see it.

He also included some pictures of one of the buildings that had been renovated into rentable accommodation and included a beautiful photograph he had taken especially for Matthew, of a field of sunflowers at sunset. All were bowing their heads except one towering sunflower in the middle of the field with huge leaves outstretched, looking upwards. Fields of sunflowers are characteristic of that part of France and, as you happen upon them, they are positively breathtaking. During daylight hours they look upwards basking in the sun's light and then bow humbly as evening falls. We used the picture as a backdrop on our computer screen and dreamed big dreams.

With the secrecy of an MI6 operation Mark went to France to view the house while I stayed with Matthew. We didn't actually tell anyone what we were up to as we wanted all available information to hand before worrying anybody with minor details, like how on earth we were going to accomplish this crazy plan! We had arranged that several people would visit Matt and me during Mark's absence so that I did not feel entirely abandoned and our Marie Curie angels were to be on duty at night. Matt was so much more stable by then and, being experienced with his care, I felt I could hold the fort for two days. Pretty watertight plan we thought...

Of course, we hadn't allowed for French air traffic control. No sooner had Mark's plane taken off from Gatwick for his destination of Bordeaux, than he opened a newspaper to read in horror that French air traffic controllers were striking the following day and all French airports would be closed. His excursion had been planned with extreme precision allowing him to be away from home for approximately forty-two hours. With the strike, it meant his return would be delayed by another twenty-four, making three days in all that I would virtually be in sole charge of our totally dependant son.

Before Mark left there was one doubt we had about the recommended viewing as there was only an acre and a half of land included. I e-mailed the agent about our reservations, and as I did so my e-mail crossed with his, telling us he had just got back from the vendors again and they had offered another three acres of land for sale with the property, but with no obligation on our part. Matt and I did our sums and quickly realised the land added up to four and a half acres!

Mark phoned me on arrival at the property. I could tell he was noticeably affected by what he saw as he used words like 'tranquil', 'stunning' and 'peaceful'. He also called me early the following morning from a beach about forty minutes away, to say he was captivated by the beauty of the place and it felt right for us to live there. The dilemma was another interested party, so he had a huge decision to make fairly promptly, well immediately actually, and without me or Matt even seeing our prospective new home. To buy or not to buy?

We bought!

In France, once you have shaken hands on a deal, it is pretty much a done deal and you are then committed to go ahead with the purchase. Rather fortuitously we were able to pay a deposit on the property a few weeks later and secure euros at a good rate to complete the purchase, due to the generosity of Mark's grandmother Edith, who you may remember went to be with the Lord after celebrating more than one hundred years on this earth. We were enthusiastically grateful to Nanna.

Finally, in July that year, I too was able to briefly visit our new home with a girlfriend. We flew to Bordeaux and drove the hour north to St Sigismond de Claremont, a tiny hamlet close to Jonzac, in the Charente Maritime where our future home nestled peacefully in quiet countryside. It was everything Mark had conveyed and more. There was a true feeling of peace about the place. Like Mark, I envisaged Mattie getting fully well there. It even boasted a wonderful saline swimming pool where we hoped Matt would enjoy aqua-physiotherapy!

But more than that, I felt God's presence there. It was like He had gone before us to prepare it and had thought of everything. So much was already in place, including apple orchards just down the lane where the farmer grew the preferred apples for Matt's juices. We also discovered there were excellent physiotherapists within easy distance. Homeopathic remedies are freely prescribed alongside conventional treatments by many French doctors and nearby hospitals boasted consultants who expressed interest in assisting us with Matt's care.

The extra buildings still to be renovated provided ample scope for the most ambitious desire to create. We hoped to be able to rent some of the accommodation to provide a small income as well as subsidise our dream of opening the doors to other families in need. The farmhouse was large and immediately habitable with lily of the valley nestling against the stonework outside and beautiful trees dotted all over the land.

The couple selling the property were originally from Shropshire in England. Graham and Wendy had lived in Spain for about seventeen years and pastored a church there. They had moved to France less than two years before as Wendy's health, following a thrombosis, required a less hot and dry climate. They bought the farmhouse, buildings and land intending to renovate. Sadly, Wendy had been left partially sighted in one eye, so deciding the venture was more than they wanted in their latter years, they offered the main part of the estate for sale, keeping some remaining land on which to build a smaller property.

They had been praying for the right family to buy the farmhouse and outbuildings. Well, that was us, we were the right family. They were friendly, eager to hear about Matt and offered us help with his care once we moved. In the months that followed we kept regular contact. They even offered to have some land prepared in readiness for planting vegetables that we would need for juices. So we ambitiously agreed to move in March 2003 allowing them time to have their new house built and for us to arrange for the sale of our house in England.

Chapter 34

Despite our circumstances, we were understandably a little excited about our proposed move and everything we believed God had planned for us. Obviously, there was much to do and we spent the next couple of months preparing our house for sale. We had only lived there for ten months prior to Matt's illness and had achieved little headway in the way of maintenance or decoration and so we set about correcting that. God graciously gave us time to rectify that and still look after Matt. I am bemused now as to why it has always taken us ages to refurbish our previous homes when we were far less occupied. Mark assures me that the speed of that undertaking was an unrepeatable one-off!

Everyday life continued to challenge us all. Matt made some amazing progress but his body was still dealing with the effects of a life-threatening illness and he was having periods of what we believed was detoxifying and healing. Sometimes it felt like we moved two steps forward and three back, but I know that wasn't the case. I know my faith requires that I believe something before I see it materialise, and much of the time I buoyantly accepted that. But in the middle of the night – that most stressed of times – when Matt's body was still being ravaged by the effects of chemotherapy, chemicals and the biopsy, and he suffered from choking mucus or seizures, I would often throw my hands up in impatient frustration and lose the plot.

Although it was quite the reverse, it felt as if we had been in that house for the duration because we were living in it '24-7' as the saying goes. We often light-heartedly made comparisons between us and the Israelites in the Old Testament. After being delivered from captivity in Egypt, it took them forty years to get across the desert to the Promised Land – a journey that could have been physically accomplished in weeks. During that time, they moaned a lot, frequently lost their faith and focus and when things weren't going their way they cried out to God a lot, a lot, a lot! But in the end, God was faithful to His promises to them. Eventually the Promised Land did become a reality to the precious few who believed. I moaned to God frequently about our circumstances, because I did not understand why our beautiful son had to suffer for so long and I wondered if the Promised Land would ever become a reality for us.

For all my moaning, we were no nearer to understanding why our lives had taken the course they had. We knew that we were very different people than before Matt became ill and we learned invaluable lessons about God, ourselves, each other and this world. To some people, the concept of moving to France may seem irresponsible, perhaps even crazy. One thing we were certain of, we couldn't go back to being the people we were before; our experiences would never let us do that. We would always have a different perspective on life, no matter where our paths went.

Family and friends, old and new, joined us as we prayed about embarking on the next part of the adventure. We prayed that we could undertake the venture totally debt free, with no mortgage, and have enough money to renovate the outbuildings, plant vegetables, get a left-hand drive something or other big enough for Matt, us and the dogs, and to survive for at least the first twelve months. After which time we hoped to be a viable enterprise able to offer help to others in need. Mark was still on unpaid leave from his job which would take him up to January 2003 and only then would we be able to consider the options available that would best suit our family priorities. The course we now plotted was in unchartered waters and we had no tangible assurance of its success, nor whether we would arrive at our destination.

As well as putting our house on the market, we set about selling any and all assets we had in order to raise as much capital as possible. We knew that the proposed move was a mammoth task and a complete lifestyle change. We also realistically set out all the things we would need immediately to care for Matthew once we got to France. We tried to determine how he would be if he kept making the small steps of progress towards being well that he had already shown and to assess what his requirements would be for the next year or so.

It was no small undertaking, with Matthew's nursing schedule to consider, as well as everything we needed to organise to accompany our complete lifestyle change – but it kept three confined inmates creatively occupied for many a long sleepless night. We referred to our future home as our Promised Land, our Canaan. Like the Israelites in the Bible, we felt we had been in a desert for too long but now, we were filled with renwed hope for a brighter future. We also had two new family members to think about. They would need certificates, injections and passports. And French lessons! None of us actually spoke French; well Mark and I had basic lessons at school and Matt was pretty good at languages, but he had a way to go before he could speak properly at all, let alone in a foreign tongue. The dogs couldn't understand English it seemed, so French would almost certainly present difficulties for them.

Speaking of the dogs, they continued to thrive whilst

putting us all through our paces. It's funny how you don't hear horror stories about owning animals until it's far too late! Our faithful family pets were definitely training us up in the way they thought we should go. We had to change Samson's name to Louis because we found neither dog would take notice of us, possibly due to the same first letter of their names – at least that's my theory! Friends thought we needed something with a French flavour and Louis rolled off the tongue and seemed fairly appropriate. Also there was a 'King Louis' in Jungle Book so we had Simba the Lion King and King Louis, the king of the apes! Both named after royalty and both determined to live as such. Mark undertook what little training we had time for and, I have to say, they all did fairly well. I'm not too sure who was meant to be in charge though. But as we dealt with one hurdle of obedience, another would present itself to test our patience. The penny finally dropped on the house-training front, while many of the plugs on our electrical appliances were mysteriously chewed off!

One day, we had to call an engineer to replace the wiring mechanism underneath Matt's special bed as only one end went up or down that day. Mark and I stood sheepishly by as the kind, patient man spent a couple of hours under the bed fiddling with some extremely complex wires before it was working once again. How they escaped electrocution is a miracle. I had to keep looking at early photos of the cute little things to convince myself that we'd bought labrador puppies and not racehorses. The layout of the downstairs of our house made it possible for them to chase each other around and around through all the rooms making the most abominable racket. Racehorses with a relentless penchant for mischief it would seem!

One funny event is worth repeating here. Mark was doing physiotherapy with Matt, leaving his paralysed left leg hanging over the bed as usual for the blood to reach his toes. From the other side of the bed, he observed Louis licking and gently mouthing Matt's foot. He rushed over, grabbed Louis to shove him away, but bending down and forward, hit the side of his head on the footboard of Matt's bed and nearly knocked himself out. He lay down on the floor with spots dancing before his eyes. Both dogs, seeing their master in such a playful position jumped in for a good old scrap!

I entered the room to see my husband looking dazed, though no alarm bells went off at that, sporting a suspicious bruise on one side of his face and a bloody earlobe. The two kings had abdicated, probably off to cause mayhem somewhere else. As I said, you never hear the bad stories until it is far too late!

Chapter 35

Looking back over that summer at the regular newsletters we were sending out, it is easy to catch the infectious theme of hope that ran throughout. But with hindsight and closer scrutiny of our diary entries, it becomes apparent that a chain of events was in motion that would once again rock our world and alter our lives beyond recognition.

Although Matthew was making what appeared to be small steps of progress, to us watching each miniscule change in every twenty-four hour period, they seemed like giant leaps. We had witnessed our son desperately ill and incapacitated for so long that any improvement in his condition was glaringly noticeable and welcomed by us. With hindsight I think we made ourselves focus on the progress whilst we dealt with the awfulness of the situation because it was the only way we could continue to function. We had long ago been stretched to our limits of endurance and during that summer I believe we knew we couldn't go any further down, so we concentrated on going up.

Realistically though our lives were being lived out on a seesaw of events and emotions. In one week, we wrote in the diary that Matt had a great day and was in his wheelchair in the warm shady garden while Mark did a bit of weeding. Another day he was sick following breakfast and lunch, contrasting with the next day when we were treated to him punching his arm out and smiling. He seemed to be sleeping well, yet also experienced whole sleepless nights.

His skin, hair and eyes looked extraordinarily healthy and yet he seemed to be losing more weight. He appeared to be peaceful and comfortable one day then uncomfortable the next, making small whimpering noises and even registering a slight temperature.

It was difficult to know what to think or do for the best. Chris and Sally from the Trust assured us that the weight loss was following a regular pattern they had witnessed with other patients on the same treatment as Matthew. In fact many were much thinner despite being up and about everyday. I think because, early on, we had experienced days and even weeks on end of terrible sickness, seizures and a host of other sufferings, as they abated to a greater degree, we coasted through what seemed less frenetic days grateful for any lull in the storm.

After much deliberation we finally decided to have the Hickman Line removed from Matt's chest. There were several reasons for this. His weekly blood tests regularly showed excellent results. He no longer seemed to need the emergency medication for any seizures that was administered by injection and the position of the line was restrictive for his day-to-day comfort and afforded an ongoing threat of infection. At one point we noticed that blood had seeped back into the actual line from his vein – something we had not seen before – and in view of his stability, decided that it was time for the line to go. It had been an advantage for a while, which we now felt had outlived its usefulness.

Although these lines are put in under general anaesthetic and are usually removed in the same way, some are accidentally pulled out by younger patients and no harm is suffered. Obviously, that is not the preferred method, as there is a cuff placed on the inside of the chest skin to hold it in place, and accidental removal can cause bleeding and discomfort and we had been briefed on leaving hospital how to cope should that situation arise. Matt occasionally caused us concern when he waved his good arm around indiscriminately as there was always the possibility that he might catch the line and just keep pulling.

We did enquire as to whether this procedure could be carried out under local anaesthetic and, if that were the case, if there was any possibility it could be undertaken at home as we were reluctant to subject Matt to a hospital visit. We didn't feel he would benefit from either the experience or the exposure to the outside world and more particularly the hospital and an ever-present threat of infection. Unfortunately, the doctors were not prepared to perform the removal at home so we had to consider the logistics of Matt visiting the hospital as an outpatient for the day.

Our furry housemates continued to provide us with daily entertainment. I admit now it was a brave venture taking on not one but two puppies in our unique circumstances. Don't believe anyone who insists that two dogs are just as easy to look after as one; they are definitely double the trouble. The only difference may be quieter nights because they have each other for company, but there is twice as much mayhem during waking hours and you haven't got a clue who the culprit is half the time.

One day they discovered our garage could be accessed through the utility room, which was frequently in use as it was the hub of preparation for all Matt's juices and the equipment needed to look after him was stored there. Whilst juicing Mark took his eyes off them for a minute and chubby brown Louis went missing. We searched high and low for him, calling all the while and ably assisted by his chum – but to no avail. Although Simba did firmly ensconce himself by the garage door, it was some time before I ventured in there to collect some more bed sheets, noticing the garage and utility room open.

Simba just kept staring into the dark unknown of the garage. With my curiosity roused I stood looking too, but sensing nothing untoward was about to close the door when the tiniest sound of movement came from a big sack of puppy food lying on its side. I stood motionless for a few more seconds and was rewarded by more shuffling sounds. Examination of the bag produced one chubby puppy with an extremely extended tummy! Exactly how much Louis devoured in the time he spent undetected in the bag will forever remain a mystery but, suffice it to say, even he could not eat his dinner and remained poleaxed under Matt's bed for the remainder of the day.

Simba's reason for living is to play. If he has a toy he is the most contented of dogs, as long as someone is playing with him that is. If Louis declines he will pester anyone else to tug, throw or tease with his latest acquisition. Louis, by contrast, is governed totally by his stomach. If it is full he is happy and on the look out for more; if it is empty he is not happy and on the urgent lookout for more! After his binge we made sure the garage door was kept firmly closed.

Chapter 36

Every spare moment in September was taken up decorating the house ready to market it. Even so, it took a long time, as Matt was our primary concern and neither of us liked being away from him for too long. But when he slept, one of us would stay by his bed and the other one would charge around performing great feats of decoration, resembling 'Changing Rooms', but sadly lacking their enviable behind-the-scenes team of assistants.

Mark's birthday that month was a gloriously sunny day and he and I celebrated a milestone as we walked into our nearby town for a frothy coffee, leaving our Marie Curie angel Heather, looking after our precious boy. It was the first outing we had made together in seventeen months. It felt extremely odd to be thus occupied and though we made an effort to linger, we found ourselves feeling more comfortable when headed once again for home. There would be time for all of that, we told ourselves, when Mattie was stronger and we were able to partake of a coffee in France.

We were both acutely aware that throughout the entire time Matthew was ill, both in and out of hospital, we were totally blessed with the most amazing help and generosity from family, friends and strangers alike. Without that support, some organised, some impromptu, there is no way we could have survived as we did. There were no adequate words to express our gratitude for every kind act that people performed for us during those painful days.

Everyone who knew of our situation also talked about us to everyone else and so news of our son's plight spread far and wide. Our plans to move to another country were accompanied by the inevitable knowledge that we would be placing ourselves beyond reasonable range of that aid.

But still people surprised us with their love and generosity. Amidst plans for Matt's line to be removed we were astonished when Rhiannon, another of our Marie Curie angels, offered the services of her neighbour Rod and his private ambulance to take us all to the hospital. He also offered to wait there during the line removal and bring us all back home again afterwards. His ambulance, a converted people carrier, was luxurious compared to any we had used before and Matthew could travel lying in comfort, with one of us next to him. It was the perfect solution to some of our concerns about the proposed venture.

In an attempt to make the process as stress free as possible for Mattie, we approached the doctors to request that Mark remain constantly with him while the line was removed under local anaesthetic. We were given permission and, because he was no longer on any chemical drugs as we had successfully discontinued all the anti-seizure medication, we asked that he be given the minimum dose of anaesthetic necessary to prevent an unfavourable reaction. When our bodies are detoxified of chemical substances, they are extremely sensitive to even the smallest amount. As back-up we had Sally prepare an emergency homeopathic kit to administer in case Matt did suffer any pain, side-effects from the anaesthetic or indeed the whole experience.

One day in late September, confident of Matt's overall stability, Mark was tempted out to play a game of golf with a friend some distance away. I undertook the afternoon's care alone and enjoyed just being with my son. We chatted about anything and everything – well, I did and Mattie was gracious enough to stay awake. Simba had recently and meticulously chewed through our phone wire, but fortunately I had a mobile always on hand. By then Matt was only having monthly blood tests, but it was still necessary for the Hickman Line to be flushed on a weekly basis to prevent any blood clotting or possible infection occurring. On that afternoon however, as the line was flushed for what would be the last time, he exhibited a number of worrying symptoms.

He seemed pale after the line flush and his hands, face and feet were uncharacteristically cold. I was relieved when Mark got home and we called Sally over for some advice. She thought he may have had a reaction to the chemicals used to flush his line. His breathing had become quite fast and he was making small sounds as if he was in pain or discomfort. We had no way of knowing exactly what was troubling him, but the symptoms continued into the evening and he had no sleep that night. Mark and I finally fell into an exhausted sleep in the early hours of the morning, either side of his bed, and when we started awake some time later, we were more than relieved to see that his breathing had returned to normal and he was sleeping.

He slept on and off for much of that day, but his system was obviously trying to deal with something unusual as his bowel movements were frequent, loose and oddly coloured. He was also moving his tongue around his mouth in an odd manner. It was so frustrating not being able to have him communicate with us and fatigue did little to ease the pressure of constantly having to nurse Matt but, miraculously by the end of the second day, he was looking really well. His continuing tongue movements still puzzled us but we put it all down to adverse effects of the line flushing and prayed that his body was in the process of removing dead cancer cells instigated and assisted by the treatment he was receiving.

My birthday came and went at the beginning of October and more friends visited to ensure that we had brief intermissions from our intense schedule. The monthly visit from the physiotherapist revealed that Matt's left hand seemed stiffer than last time, and his sleeping pattern was a little erratic, but no serious alarm bells were sounding. We were able to sit him up on the bed again during the weekly physio's visit that month and then on the 15th October, following a calm, though not altogether sleep-filled night, we set off just before seven in the morning for the hospital.

Matt was made comfortable on the portable stretcher and Mark sat next to him in the ambulance holding his hand while I rode shotgun up front. It was very strange and quite frightening to be going back into a hospital environment with all the garish lights, noise, contrasting temperatures and all too familiar sights. But this time, as we wheeled Matthew through the endless corridors, Mark and I felt a confidence that eluded us during his extended hospital stay. We no longer felt like reluctant participants in circumstances beyond our control.

It was interesting answering questions for the inevitable mountain of forms to be completed. One of the doctors asked me to confirm that Matt was suffering from melanoma on the brain. I told her we weren't sure anymore as he had outlived the prognosis by a vast amount of time and seemed to be doing fairly well. She looked at me indulgently and wrote purposefully on the form 'cranial melanoma'. We were frequently asked what medication Matt was on for the seizures and we reiterated he had not been on any for months. I'm not sure how that transferred onto their forms, but their facial expressions were somewhere between disbelief and amazed surprise.

Chapter 37

Matthew was at the front of the queue for treatment that morning only to be displaced in the event of an emergency. So by eight-thirty he'd had lots of reassurance from us and some herbal medicine to help with anxiety and possible pain and we were on our way to theatre. We explained that in the event of Matt becoming anxious, we had some tried and tested natural remedies that Mark could administer. The surgeon and anaesthetist stated their preference to go with what they knew, listing the drugs they proposed to inject into Matthew if, in their opinion, it was required. We both felt scared and so prayed in earnest. I remained outside while Mark went in to be gowned up, only then to be informed by the surgeon that hospital protocol prevented anyone accompanying a patient into the theatre itself and he was to remain outside the room, unable to see or touch Matt.

It was both frustrating and disturbing because when we last spoke with the anaesthetist we believed he had given his permission for Mark to be with Matt at all times but was obviously overridden by the surgeon. Mark had a tense moment of decision – to question the ruling and appeal, perhaps causing problems, or to say nothing. He quickly offered up a prayer that, above all, Matt would remain calm and seizure-free, requiring nothing other than the slightest local anaesthetic, and that he would feel no pain.

That's exactly what seemed to transpire and twenty minutes later we were wheeling Matthew back to his temporary room. He had a pressure bandage over the cut in his neck where the Hickman Line had entered the artery and a dressing over the exit point on his chest. We gave him some arnica immediately to help with the body's natural healing process and waited for him to be expeditiously examined and discharged.

And we waited...remembering only too clearly how inordinately slowly the wheels of paperwork in hospitals turn. Finally at eleven o'clock, the doctor on call came in accompanied by about six other personnel. She asked many of the questions we had already answered and we inevitably engaged in a conversation about Matthew's present state. Many of the doctors we encountered that day at the hospital seemed reluctant to acknowledge his small though meaningful improvements. They offered no encouragement as to why the emphatic prognosis given last year had been so long outlived and questioned whether Matthew was enjoying quality of life or just surviving. It was difficult to listen to their seeming negativity and not feel discouraged, despite our overall enthusiasm. The events of that morning reminded us all too vividly of the previous difficult months in hospital.

Although it already happens on a very small scale, we look forward to the day when there is more easy simultaneous availability of conventional and alternative therapies in caring for patients with degenerative illnesses. The purpose of any treatment or therapy is to attempt to effect a cure and it would be a great tragedy if people were not made aware of all the possibilities and encouraged to make safe, realistic choices according to their preferences. Our hope is that many people whose paths we crossed will recall a very special and courageous young man and they will remember that we do have choices when faced with terminal illnesses.

As far as we were concerned our position had not changed from the day we first received Matthew's devastating diagnosis. We wanted to do everything we possibly could to help our son and we determined, without prejudice, to investigate every available avenue and assess its merits. We'd had panic attacks, we had been scared beyond imagining, we had fought, wept and held each other tight in the bleak days and dark nights. But we kept returning to our faith. We had been tested and tried, ridiculed and intimidated but we continued to rely on God to provide us with the strength to go on and prayed to Him alone for Matthew's life. Undoubtedly, with hindsight, there are decisions we would change, but without that luxury we had to make the most of the hand we had been dealt, whether it seemed fair or not.

It was with a huge sigh of relief that we headed home in our own luxurious ambulance. After resettling Matt on his special bed, all three of us managed to enjoy a couple of hours peaceful sleep that afternoon. The three bears were back safe and sound, with baby bear in his most favourite place, between his mum and dad. But our peace was short-lived.

Chapter 38

The ink was barely dry on the newsletter we sent out to everyone worldwide who was following Matt's progress, to tell them how well the procedure had gone, when he experienced a really bad reaction to something. We couldn't be sure but assumed, along with those treating him, that it was another period of the detoxification process. It was possible that his body was reacting to the traumatic return to hospital or to the anaesthetic, as the symptoms were all similar to those he exhibited after the last line flush. Whatever the case, the situation was further complicated by the fact that he could not speak nor express what was happening to him. Now, his pupils were extremely dilated, he had a temperature, several tiny seizures and his breathing was rapid once again. I watched him constantly throughout the first night with Heather, while Mark grabbed some precious sleep in order to take over care the following day.

I remember feeling totally helpless as we witnessed Matt in such obvious discomfort, feeling that I couldn't take much more of the stress. Feelings of inadequacy that had long been suppressed rushed to the surface to accuse and condemn. We were exhausted and when he didn't sleep for the next thirty-six hours, I cried out for the nightmare to end. I just wanted my son to be all right. Eventually he fell peacefully asleep after Sally faithfully came and administered more homeopathic remedies, but he remained unwell for several days.

We continued to understand how Matthew's specialised diet gave him streamlined nutrition in the form of liquid juices, buffered with precise supplements, minerals, amino acids, vitamins and enzymes together with only natural remedies. Coupled with decontaminated water these were all designed to assist his body in destroying malignant cells and eliminating them from the body whilst facilitating the regeneration of healthy cells and tissue. It could have been this very clean state his body was in that caused him to respond rapidly to the chemical input during the recent surgery and which may have led to this latest reaction. More than ever we realised how much more disadvantaged Matthew was after the disastrous effects of his biopsy. Unable to speak or express his needs, our care for him was governed by guesswork.

The type of treatment we had embarked on was not an instant panacea. It was unlikely Matthew's illness had developed overnight, but rather evolved over a long period of time and was the result of many parts of an equation. So the healing process – bereft of any instant and miraculous act of God – might also be a long and painstaking process. Mark and I were beginning to realise the knowledge and wisdom we were gaining would be infinitely more valuable to others in similar situations than a miraculous healing. We both believed God could heal Matthew instantly, yet for reasons we did not yet fully understand, He chose to take us through a lengthy learning experience changing much of our thought processes and challenging what little we knew about the remarkable human body. Only time would reveal what use we could be to others in similar situations.

Chris Ashton promptly visited his favourite patient to allay our fears that, although Matthew seemed painfully thin to my watchful mother's eye, and was quieter, not interacting with us so much, his body, trimmed of all its excess weight and burdens was hopefully using every ounce of energy to fight his illness. He also informed us that he could still lose some more weight and remain on track with his healing process as his general behaviour was characteristic of other patients who were further along the road to recovery. It was comforting to speak to Chris; his knowledge and experience as a biochemist was invaluable in explaining to two lay people how our bodies can deal with disease given the correct assistance.

We had observed first-hand some amazing stages in Matt's development that convinced us of the truth behind Chris and Sally's statements. Several weeks before, a number of marks had appeared on Matthew's back. They were brownish marks resembling large freckles, positioned on his scalp and the back of his shoulders and neck. During the ensuing weeks, we witnessed those marks first increasing in size and number and then becoming smaller and fainter as they appeared to travel downwards on his back before almost disappearing altogether.

We learned that homeopathy treats disease by considering the whole person and using minute doses of natural substances taken largely from plants, animals or minerals. The main principle is the Law of Similars, or 'Let like be cured by like'. Substances which can produce symptoms in healthy people are capable of curing those same symptoms in sick people when administered in small enough doses. The main approach of conventional medicine differs in that it combats disease with strong doses of mainly chemical substances that have the opposite effect to the symptoms, although the principals of similars is somewhat applied in the process of vaccinations.

It is recognised in the practice of homeopathic treatment that improvement and cure in a diseased body comes from within outward, or, from more important to less important organs and the symptoms disappear from above, downward. Matthew had been diagnosed with a terminal primary melanoma on his brain affecting his entire nervous system in a seemingly advanced stage, although up to that point we had witnessed few outward signs that his body's immune system was breaking down. It made sense that if his body was in the process of any kind of healing, it could very well occur in the same manner.

When he underwent the biopsy the operating surgeon informed us, in his words, that Matthew's brain appeared brown and granular and not as healthy brain tissue. Weighing up the knowledge we had gleaned over the ensuing months and the specific changes we observed in his body and condition, led us to believe the brown pigmentation marks were connected to his original illness, and their manifestation and pattern at this point could indicate his body was undergoing a deep cleansing and repairing process.

Chris Ashton from the Trust always encouraged us, without ever misleading us to harbour false hope. As well as a serious disease, Matthew's body was having to deal with and eliminate toxins from the chemotherapy and all the chemical allopathic drugs he had been given. He believed Matt was approaching the end of this cleaning-out period and his body would soon show visible signs of the subtle healing within: healthy cells multiplying, scar tissue being repaired and his entire central nervous system being restored. Although Matt was somewhat of a trailblazer, since no one with his diagnosis and of his age had undergone this type of treatment, he was to an extent following a rough pattern of other Trust patients, many of whom, keeping rigidly to their prescribed treatment, had recovered from their illness.

Everything we attempted was a learning curve, for we

could not yet rely on Matthew communicating the vital changes he experienced. When we increased Matt's food and supplement prescription to allow for his upward growth spurt, he suffered a slight reaction then too. It was only by these trials and errors thatwe discovered the slightest alteration of practically anything we gave him, even those things we knew to be beneficial, could cause an upset as his weakened body tried to rid itself of waste matter too quickly. Some things you learn the hard way.

Also during that time Matthew's mouth seemed particularly targeted. He had brownish coloured tissue deposits resembling dried mucus inside his mouth and over his tongue which we gently removed with a damp swab when it became noticeable. That week though, saw the return of the dreaded throat mucus. It was extremely thick and gloopy and must have seemed like cling-film over his wind-pipe preventing him breathing. It caused him to retch and vomit. I share this with you to try to convey something of the relentless suffering he had to contend with. With everything else we were dealing with these additional setbacks frustrated the socks off Mark and me. But nothing is so humbling as rolling your son over as he throws up for the umpteenth time that day and yet seeing no facial sign of the quiet desperation he must have felt, unable to do anything for himself.

I still battled with a desire to stomp off somewhere in outer space, let off some lengthy primeval scream and then gradually float back to being me, but all peaceful and fluffy. Because life didn't allow that luxury I'm afraid I stomped around the house frequently letting out cries and moans, until I came back to earth with a jolt realising how difficult it must have been for our teenage son who had been in a bed for nineteen months. He had to accept the hand that had been dealt to him and live with it without even being able to vocalise his feelings. With hindsight I wish I could have taken a leaf from my son's book and tried to handle adversity with his dignity and graciousness.

There was a part of me that wanted to shout that it wasn't fair that he had been in bed for that long, missing out on so much – playing games, seeing friends, just hanging out being a teenager. There was part of me that died every time I saw one of his mates and realised that I needed to look upwards to make eye contact. There was a part of me that wanted to hear what all his friends were up to and yet recoiled inwardly like a wounded animal when I heard minute details of their lives. There was a part of me that felt as if my husband, my son and myself were in a prison without locks, a place without time, a situation without sense, a sentence with no reprieve.

However bad it was for us, I had to keep reminding myself that Matthew was the patient and the focus was on him, not me. He had to rely on us for his every need. He couldn't speak properly, he seldom cried out, he wasn't able to say he'd had enough or give a primeval scream and then lay back all peaceful and fluffy. There was still a part of me that wanted to shout "Unfair!", that would do anything to alleviate his pain, that wanted to turn back the clock, rewind time to the split second before the first rogue cell multiplied itself in our son's brain. But this was our 'groundhog day'. One day my Bible reading talked about my prison door being open because Jesus won my freedom for me at Calvary. The house and our situation would only feel like prison if we gave in to our fears and let it become as such. My faith provided me with good sound advice; I wondered why in reality it was often so difficult to put that advice into practice.

Did you know, the African impala can jump ten feet high and cover a distance of ten yards in one leap? Yet this magnificent animal can be confined within walls only three feet high. Why? Because unless it first sees where it will land, it's afraid to jump. Faith is the ability to jump and trust God, even when you can't see. It opens doors and frees you from every prison of fear. Jesus had already freed Matthew, Mark and me...we were not imprisoned, I prayed we'd have the faith to fight fear and jump when the time came.

Chapter 39

The puppies continued to bless and stretch us. With hindsight I think it was good that we had them though, as their affable natures provided companionship and fun for us all and their excellent impersonations of teenagers with attitude kept us entertained. They stalked around the place like intimidating hyenas, continually on the lookout for mischief. Woe betide anyone who left anything lying around that was valuable, edible or useful. It was swiftly disposed of by the brat pack. Again I lost count of the number of people who mentioned how brave we were to get two puppies at exactly the same time – especially two labrador puppies! Grateful for those timely reminders, we vowed to consider the advice before getting any more!

However, they were a good excuse for Mark and me to take turns and get out of the house for half an hour or so each day. There were several good walks close by and still some blue sky to be enjoyed as October's warm autumnal shades made way for November's wintry ensemble. Mark used his time to pray and enjoy the solitude. I usually listened to tapes for the course on homeopathy I was studying then. Both dogs liked lounging in the fading rays of sun that fell across our garden. They loved sitting in the sunshine – so hopefully France would suit them too. We looked forward hopefully. There was still no sign of a buyer for the house, but I agreed to leave that minor detail to God; I'd got enough to think about. I did wonder though if He knew much about the property market in the Thames Valley!

Throughout those new reactions Matt suffered, he had taken to holding both his arms very tightly bent up against his chest. Ordinarily, we should have been pleased that he was moving his otherwise inert left arm, but we were a little concerned because both arms seemed to be very rigidly held in that position and would remain so for as long as we allowed. It took a great deal of gentleness and reassurance to place one down by his side and even then he would quickly pull it back towards himself. In fact his entire upper body seemed unusually stiff and uncomfortable. As a result of his behaviour, he was much stiffer to manipulate during the physio exercises. Our concern about that and his still dwindling weight played heavily on our minds but his inability to communicate with us meant that we were reduced to being observers of his condition rather than being able to take preventative measures.

We continued to place him in the wheelchair most days and to us at the time his condition and progress seemed to continue much as it had for many months. With hindsight we realise that there was a very gradual deterioration over a couple of weeks, but then we either did not fully realise what was happening because Matt couldn't assist us verbally, or we confused the outward signs with the detoxifying process we knew was going on inside his body. He suffered once more from diarrhoea and again his bottom became very red and sore from the effects of that, in spite of our diligent checks and frequent changes. More undignified treatment for Mattie to bear.

Interspersed with these added symptoms, which to us were worrying and frustrating but to Matthew must have been extremely hard to endure given his weakened state, there were days when he seemed much improved and more like his old self. Again he was sleeping well one night and wide awake for the entirety of the next. But he usually seemed to catch up on his sleep during the morning and seemed cognisant afterwards.

Halfway through November 2002 Sally, our homeopath, and her husband left England to return to her native New Zealand. We had known for some time that she was leaving, but nothing really prepared us for the sadness at their departure. They loved Matt and had become our friends alongside Sally's professional services. We saw them on their last evening before they set off on their extended journey home via Tibet and the Far East. Although we kept telling ourselves everything Matt needed was already in place, it seemed there was the shadow of a black cloud on our horizon and we felt somewhat alone.

We decided to move his bed from our lounge, through adjoining doors, to what was originally the dining room which had a connecting serving hatch to the kitchen and the utility room. We had also done it some weeks previously to give Mattie a change of scenery. We were ever aware that he had been ensconced in bed in the lounge for seventeen months with only brief excursions to wherever we could wheel him in his chair. From his new vantage point, he could see us better if we were in the kitchen preparing his diet and we could watch him closely, talking to him constantly through the hatch. The room had good memories. Before the onset of his illness he had claimed it for his den. He enjoyed entertaining his friends in there. It was cosy and they would often conveniently open the serving hatch and request something from the all-day menu!

We enjoyed a memorable visit from my family that month as my niece had just given birth to a little boy and she was eager to introduce him to his 'Uncle Matt'. With my sister, my brother-in-law and her husband we spent the afternoon crammed into his den taking pictures of Matthew with his new baby cousin. Matt always took time to spend with younger children and he loved babies. It was hard to live in the present at times like that and not hanker after a past that was gone forever and headed towards a future unknown.

As it transpired, on Monday 18th November, having spoken to Chris at the Trust, we called our GP in to take a throat swab from Mattie as our concern for the residue that kept forming in his mouth was growing and we wondered if he had an infection there. Even though we were regularly cleaning it, the small scab-type formations were worrying as they showed signs of bleeding and if loosened they might drop down his throat and cause him to choke. We were also able to catch a rare glimpse of his tonsils and observed they were red and looked sore. Our doctor came, looked Matt over, took a swab and left without raising any undue alarm.

Although he slept well on the Monday night he had cried out in his sleep. Rhiannon and Mark covered the shift that night. In the morning, the roof of his mouth was coated in a sticky green substance and he appeared to have some white patches, that resembled ulcers, forming. Liaising with Chris at the Trust, we sought to find a homeopathic remedy that might assist Matt, but he did not seem well that day suffering sweats, sickness and a small seizure.

By the Wednesday morning we were all shattered as Matt hadn't slept at all again during the night so neither had we. His eyes were unnaturally wide open and quite bloodshot. His breathing was accelerated again. We were in almost constant contact with Chris by phone as he sought ways to ease Matt's suffering. By the afternoon he had only closed his eyes for seconds at a time and was considerably weakened. Another night was spent with us both on constant duty by his bedside, and it was obvious something was not right.

Chapter 40

The following day passed in a blur of intense nursing, changing Matt, and trying to comfort him and ourselves. Tempers were fraught as the sleep deficit got larger and we were pushed once again to the limits of our endurance in trying to help our beloved son. His breathing was still laboured and it was difficult to give him any of his essential feed or juices as he seemed so unwell and weak. Mark and I took it in turns to stay awake with him throughout that Thursday night whilst the other one tried to get some sleep on one of the beds in the lounge. Several times I dozed, exhausted in the chair during my shifts and awoke to tiny whimpers from my son. It was very distressing to see him like that and my roughly patched and plastered heart felt like it was fracturing all over again.

We kept praying, whilst doing everything we possibly could to ease his discomfort. But we were so caught up in the urgency of caring for him that we neglected to call in any other assistance and just soldiered on. Fortunately Heather came again on the Friday morning as part of her day shift for us. It was a blessing to have someone else there, as Mark and I were very close to collapse. Matt became more stable and things didn't seem so desperate in the light of day. The doctors' surgery called and said that the lab results from the swab showed a slight presence of bacteria in Matt's throat, but no more than most people would carry. Olivia, our other nurse, came that Friday night and Mark again did back-up, sending me upstairs to bed to get some sleep. I left some new homeopathic remedies, to be given to Mattie during the course of the night, in the hope that they may help him through this latest crisis.

Notwithstanding the fact that I could hardly keep my eyes open, I still found it difficult to get to sleep that night. But I must have eventually drifted off as, after what seemed only a short time, Olivia was in my bedroom calling my name. I sat up in bed and listened as she told me it was six o'clock and I had better come down straight away as we had a very poorly little boy downstairs. My heart almost stopped as I quickly put on some clothes and rushed downstairs. One look at Mark's tired and drawn face made my stomach do somersaults with fear.

If it were possible, Matt seemed to have lost even more weight overnight. His head looked minute on the pillow. His eyes were bloodshot and his cheeks were drawn in pain. Both arms were bent up tight against his chest and he didn't have to speak to convey to me what he was going through. I just wanted to crumple in a heap and cry until this horrible nightmare went away. Instead, I gave him what natural remedies I was able to but with my limited knowledge I felt helpless to do anything for my most precious child. Olivia stayed beyond the end of her shift to help us, finally leaving at nine o'clock when we phoned Chris Ashton for help and advice. He was unable to get to the house due to prior urgent engagements that morning but was in constant contact by phone.

As that Saturday progressed, the diarrhoea got steadily worse until it was almost constant and Matt was also being sick. He had become too weak to cough and clear the mucus that was at the back of his throat and we gently turned him on his side from time to time so that it could drain from his mouth. Neither of us was able to leave his bedside during the copious sheet changes or for fear of him choking as he was sick. It was frightening to observe what was happening and not be able to do anything that seemed to ease his suffering.

As we undertook every task that was required, so wrapped up in trying to help Matt we both withdrew inside ourselves, voicing little of our own personal suffering as we battled to cope with each agonising passing hour. We made a brief call to good friends to request that they come and help us overnight, as we soon realised we had neither the strength nor ability to be alone for the coming night. Helene and Patrick made arrangements for their two children to be looked after and quickly drove the sixty miles from their house to ours arriving in the late afternoon.

The sense of relief that someone else was going to be there with us for that night was overwhelming. We were just grateful for their love and concern but as soon as Helene saw Mattie she expressed her anxiety over his chest. As he breathed now there were low rattling sounds and she was concerned in case it was something more sinister than just mucus. Declining to call strangers on the doctor's emergency contact number we instead called Diane, our weekly physiotherapist, and she visited on her way out early that evening to look at Matt and see if some very gentle movements would shift the build-up in his chest and throat.

We discontinued his juices, feeds and all his supplements as the sickness increased and just concentrated on making him as comfortable as possible. It was extremely hard because every five or ten minutes we would have to change his pants and the sheets which became quickly soiled. Everything was infinitely easier to accomplish with four people and we even managed to have something to eat because thoughtful friends from church, not even aware of the gravity of our situation that day, delivered supper to our house. Miraculously, like the loaves an fishes, it was sufficient to feed four grateful adults that evening.

Later that night, things worsened slightly so we arranged sleeping shifts to maximise everyone's usefulness and ensure we all got some rest. Mark and Patrick took the first watch, while Helene and I disappeared upstairs to try to sleep. It was hard to switch off from all that was going on downstairs, as Mattie was having small seizures on top of everything else. But we both knew the guys were more than capable of caring for him and would wake us if we were needed. We talked nervously for a while and then finally fell asleep for a couple of hours until about four in the morning.

As we ventured back downstairs, we were hopeful that perhaps the boys had all experienced a peaceful night, as they had not come to wake us before time but, on entering the room, the looks on their faces quickly told us that the situation was really grave and Matthew had worsened. He was being almost constantly sick and the diarrhoea had not abated. His fragile body looked skeletal. My whole body was numb. After nineteen months of seesawing emotions and indescribable heartache I didn't think it was possible to experience any deeper pain, but I did in those bleak pre-dawn hours. Even to my untrained eyes, it seemed that Matt's life was fading away – as if his body had already begun to close down and there was just a tiny thread of life inside him hanging onto this world.

Helene and I were silently sobbing as we took over his care, leaving the men free to go upstairs to rest. They looked done in; we all were. We didn't know what was going to happen or when, but we did know that the situation could not continue for much longer in its intensity. We took it in turns to clean Mattie while the other one stayed in view of his face, talking softly to him all the time, telling him how loved he was, how special he was and how brave he was.

Holding my son's tiny, thin head as the sickness continued I thought my heart would explode with the pain. His body trembled occasionally with a small seizure and I silently pleaded with God, "Enough, please, enough." I stroked his hand and his cheek gently; he was so weak I was afraid I might hurt him just by touching him. Then I felt a strange feeling around us. It is difficult to put into words but it felt bright in the room although the dawn light outside was pale and dim. I spoke to Matt and asked him if he could see the light. "It's Jesus, sweetheart," I said. "Mattie, if He takes your hand, go with Him my darling. I love you with all my heart, but He loves you more. Take His hand if He asks you." I could not stop the flow of tears and as I looked at Helene – I realised neither could she. It seemed our son was barely with us then and so I went and woke Mark, even though he had slept for one short hour. I was afraid Mattie might leave us without his daddy by his side.

MOTHER'S POEM

There are no words that I can say to ease your pain or
hide away your failing dreams, your broken bones,

I have no words to change this day.

Helpless child I'll hold your hand and wipe your brow,
I'll wash away your every stain, all this pain.

I will hold you in my arms again.

From your first breath I loved you so. And with this love
I'll let you go. Now breathe your last my precious child,

It is time for me to guide you home.

Anonymous

Chapter 41

You may wonder, reading this, why we did not call the doctor or an ambulance in view of the gravity of the situation. I know I am, but I have to keep reminding myself that I am seeing events now with hindsight. I believe at that point we both would have done anything to prevent Matthew from suffering further, but to call the doctor or an ambulance would have meant instant admission to hospital along with all the paraphernalia accompanying that decision. Wheels would have begun turning that we would have been unable to stop. When we left the hospital in Oxford, we were told that our son was terminally ill with an untreatable disease and we were allowed to take him home to nurse him until he died. Our faith gave us courage to undertake that mammoth task, whilst we hoped, prayed and believed for a miraculous healing.

In making the choice to do that and to proactively try alternative treatments and remedies, we then placed ourselves beyond the knowledge and limitations of the conventional medical profession. Although we received community backup help, it was not generally considered by them that anything we were undertaking would make any difference to the outcome of his original prognosis. He had been diagnosed with cranial melanoma and given a maximum of three months to live. If Matt was returned to conventional hospital methods they would use machines to breathe for him and keep him alive but their original diagnosis would not alter. They might pump him full of antibiotics and a plethora of other chemical drugs to try to treat his immediate condition but, by their own admission, they had no new treatment that could save his life.

Mark and I had the most agonising decision of all to make that Sunday morning. When we learned the medical profession could do nothing more for our son, we chose to explore all other available options – not putting our faith in any particular drugs or treatments, nor any specific diet or supplements, but in God alone. As I said long ago in that tiny hospital room, when we were told of our son's condition, if God chose to use conventional medicines, that was fine, if He chose to use alternative therapies, that too was fine and if He chose to miraculously heal Matt without any of those things, that was also fine. But having made the choice to go down the road we did, we didn't feel we could change our minds and put Matt through another painful and impersonal period of hospitalisation. He had already endured too much in his courageous battle. We will have to live with all the decisions we made and trust that we did everything we possibly could at the time for our darling boy, without the benefit of hindsight.

Writing this now seems hard because everything inside me is screaming, "Why didn't we take him to hospital earlier that week? Why didn't we allow him to be taken even as late as that Sunday morning?" But it is important to view this as we did at the time it happened. As I said at the beginning, to look at things with hindsight is misleading and deceptive. Mark and I have discussed this issue at considerable length, as you may imagine, and both of us have said we did not realise the severity of Matthew's condition earlier that week. But then apparently neither did our general practitioner when she visited on the Monday. Throughout the time we nursed him, living in the same room and observing him closely twenty-four hours a day, we saw him experience many periods of crises. He had been critically ill on more than one occasion but had made remarkable recoveries. There was little at the beginning of that week, or even as late as the Friday, to alert us into believing that he would not bounce back from that latest setback.

As soon as we could, we placed an emergency call to our doctor. She arrived promptly and examined Matt informing us that he had pneumonia and was very, very ill. She offered to arrange for him to go to hospital for antibiotics. But, as I said, wheels would begin to turn that we could not stop and we knew he would inevitably be on a life-support machine again. She suggested we administer the powerful anti-seizure drugs we had for emergencies, but on examination we found them all to be out of date, with the exception of a paraldehyde pessary. Agonisingly, we both decided not to give that to Matt.

I think we were both relieved that we did not have the option to administer any of the other drugs. Paraldehyde is a flammable and powerful nervous system depressant with a very disagreeable odour. We had witnessed its alarming properties in the Oxford hospital when it had melted the container it was in before being administered to Matthew as a pessary. We both declined its use that morning knowing it would cause Matt more pain. We asked the doctor what his chances of recovery were, even in hospital. She did not think he would live for very much longer. So the hardest decision we would ever be expected to make seemed suddenly to be taken from our hands.

We were all crying as we decided that we would keep our promise made to a remarkably brave and special young man some seventeen months before. We would not take him back to hospital. When the doctor left we all sat around Mattie's bed and prayed. I quickly sent out an e-mail to everyone worldwide who had been praying for him, for them to join us in asking for God's mercy however severe it may seem.

I cannot pretend it wasn't torturous to watch him during the last hour of his life on this earth and only God can heal us all of those stark and painful images etched in our minds. Jesus came and took our darling boy home to be with Him at one-fifty that afternoon, Sunday November 24th 2002. He was thirteen years and eleven months old. He had a small seizure and Mark waited for it to finish before he continued reading to him from his treasured Youth Bible. We were both by his side as Jesus took his hand and led him home. We were broken and left behind but we knew he was finally safe in the arms of the One who loved him even more than us. As we watched his heart stop beating and his chest fall for the last time, all four of us held our breath, as it seemed time stood still.

Chapter 42

My memories about the remainder of that day are conflicting. On the one hand time seemed to pass in a blur, yet I can recall certain things that happened in minute detail. The best description I can give is one of a numbness that rendered me able to see, hear and function like an automaton but when emotions did surface they seemed diluted, hardly reflecting the torturous pain consuming my inside; I had withdrawn into that state of self-preservation in order to survive. I was waiting for something to jolt me out of an awful dream. It was like falling and falling yet, though my body could feel the strangeness of falling, I never hit the ground. I erected safe imaginary tramlines that day within the confines of which I existed and they stayed with me for a long time. It is amazing how our bodies continue to exist in times of trauma without us knowingly being aware of all the complexities involved. Is it survival at the most primitive level?

It was probably a minute before anyone moved as we all stood transfixed watching the place on Mattie's chest where his heart was. A kind of disbelief hung over us all because we so wanted it to begin beating again. But it didn't and that area of skin quickly became discoloured like a bruise. Then I was aware of Mark, Patrick and Helene crying out and someone saying, "No, no!" But I could neither speak, nor cry out. Instead I moved into a detached organising mode. I covered Matt's little body up as Mark tenderly closed his eyes. Then I remember us tidying up in the room and performing unimportant tasks. Some time after, Mark and I stood alone with Matt and prayed our biggest prayer for him to miraculously come back from the dead. He didn't and I'm not sure if what we felt was utter grief, inconsolable disappointment or exhausted resignation. We didn't exchange many words, relying instead on our recently acquired silent communication with each other that spoke volumes.

We called the doctor back, as she needed to witness Mattie's death. I clearly remember her asking if we had an undertaker in mind. I heard Mark, in shocked surprise say, 'no' because we hadn't expected Matthew to die, let alone consider arrangements for that possibility. Were we deluded? With hindsight, had we been living in a fantasy world? I do not believe so. But I do believe with hindsight we view events in continuous motion and so are able to see patterns, common threads and thereby seem only too wise. I have resurrected every agonising decision we made throughout Matt's illness and his last days with us. Every second has been carefully placed under my exacting microscope, until I could see no more through scalding tears. And my conclusion? With hindsight? In everything, we did what we truly believed was the best for our son at that time and in those unique circumstances. Looking back there are some things I would change if I had the time over again, but that is a seductive thought that only lures me into thinking we and not God can alter the course of our lives.

I spent some time alone with my son, tucking him up properly, and kissing his beautiful, familiar face. I remember thinking how long his fingers were and how tapered his fragile hands. His skin was still warm and I am pleased because it was the last time I would hug him on this earth and I wanted to remember the warmth of his body. He looked so still, peaceful yet so empty and I knew that although his earthly body was all I had to picture my son, he had no further need for it. His spirit was free with his precious Jesus and he was in no more pain or discomfort. Our son was finally home and on the biggest adventure ever, but without his daddy or me.

When the gentlemen arrived from the undertakers, I distinctly remember running around looking for Matt's Youth Bible which we suddenly couldn't find. He and Mark had used it so much, right up to the end and it was all dog-eared but we wanted to keep it with him. We can only assume that in the blur of tidying up, it must have been thrown out with some soiled linen. We were asked if there was anything special we would like to include in the casket with him. We made sure that he had his favourite colourful bracelets to adorn his wrists for the last time. One had WWJD printed on it. It stood for 'What Would Jesus Do', another had FROG on it and stood for 'Fully Rely On God' and the third one displayed PUSH which meant 'Pray Until Something Happens'. They were all popular with the young people in church and Matt was seldom seen without them when he was well; he had always worn them with pride.

It was extremely difficult to watch them prepare Matthew's body to go to the Chapel of Rest. Although we knew his spirit was no longer inhabiting his earthly body, as his mother it was painfully hard to entrust my baby to the care of anyone else. I had given birth to him looked after him all his life and, with Mark, tenderly and lovingly nursed him for over nineteen months and I wasn't sure I wanted anyone else to touch him now or take him away from me. But those feelings were a natural reaction to letting go, I'm sure. We had good friends with us who didn't offer any trite answers to the many questions that bombarded our minds, they just loved us through that strangely surreal time.

For the rest of the day and well into the evening, we sat huddled into our small study. Joined by another willing friend for a time and then my sister and with only one computer chair, one armchair and the floorspace to accommodate us all, we found it strangely comforting to be close together. We chatted for hours, often laughing at wonderful memories we had of Matthew. We chose to remain cocooned in a time warp, where decisions could be shelved and we could shun the outside world and all that entailed and just exist for a short time on an eiderdown of feathers. There would be plenty of time to come when we would have to face the reality of life without our beloved only son, but for a time at least, we were safe in the past.

Chapter 43

My sister, along with our friends, stayed for the next few days, surrounding us with tangible, loving support, frequent hugs and ensuring we remembered to eat and could walk without wobbling. That night Mark and I finally drifted into sleep – the first time we were both in the same bed at the same time in over nineteen months. We held each other's arms and hands so tight, fearing to let go in case we plunged into blackness and lost the remaining shred of security we had left.

I think I was the first one awake in the house early the following morning. I lay in bed aware of a searing pain seeping up my legs, almost as if my skin was slowly being peeled off – yet the pain was deep inside, not on the surface. It continued on up to my stomach and chest and then I heard the most agonising sound, like an animal caught viciously in a trap. I slowly realised it was me but I could not stop until Mark woke up and we just clung to each other for ages, sobbing.

The days immediately following Matt's death continued in a jumble of memories and conflicting emotions. One minute we could be having a normal conversation, the next would bring a flood of tears, the next anger, though more often frequent bouts of silent, excruciating pain. I suppose our extreme capriciousness was an expression of the shock and grief we felt unable to express. Sleep became a reluctant bedfellow for us both especially in the early hours of the morning. Waking from forgetful slumber was particularly painful as within those first few seconds reality flooded in without mercy.

We walked the puppies – needing to yet grudgingly, finding little solace in the routine. What was once an opportunity to escape the relentless indoor regime had now become a necessary chore. But at least as we walked we talked together and were scathingly honest about our feelings. The paradox was that it was only days since his death and yet it seemed we had already lived a lifetime since he was with us. Our time, so full before caring for Matt, now tormented us as it stretched endlessly, achingly before us, taunting us with huge empty voids.

Looking back I realise that dreamlike state continued for quite a while. We drew some comfort in making plans to hold a celebration of Matthew's life when we buried his body and so extended the invitation to anyone who wished to come. Because many of our friends either lived or worked abroad, the date was set for eleven days later, December 5th, in order to give as many people as possible the opportunity to attend. I believe planning the event kept Mark and I alive, focused and sane. Alongside our plans to move to France we had been in the throes of setting up a Trust Fund not only to help Matt, but for the purpose of helping other children in similar circumstances after our move. We requested no floral tributes, apart from close family and welcomed any donations to be used for that and other children's charities we knew would be close to Matthew's heart.

Friends from church generously offered their talents, technical and artistic services, as we co-ordinated the funeral and time of thanksgiving for Matthew's wonderful though tragically short life. We carefully chose a selection of music, particular favourites of his, that meant all the more to us now and we asked many of his friends and young people at church to participate, either by playing or singing in the band, reading something or praying special prayers. Understandably, not all of them felt able to do anything demonstrative on the day and there were a few that could not bring themselves to attend in their grief. We realised everyone who knew Matt bore their own version of pain.

As soon as we were able we visited Matthew's body at the Chapel of Rest. Everyone involved there was especially caring and sensitive to our situation and we made several visits over the ensuing days. I find it difficult to verbally express what I felt about the encounter as the whole experience touched emotions deep inside myself. Although it gave me a more serene image of Matt after all the suffering he had endured in those last days, it was not in any way easy. But with hindsight I am glad I went to see him, and in an odd way I felt we were still connected with him physically. Comforting though it was to see him looking peaceful, it was somewhat disconcerting as his heavy-lashed eyelids looked about to flutter open, allowing his blue eyes to grace us with their piercing beauty, and it was easy to believe that his characteristic smile would once more chase around his lips. It never occurred to us to ask anyone about the experience beforehand and the coldness of his skin to my touch brought a terrifying finality to our circumstances that made my heart pound fearfully as I cried out to God for reassurance that this was not the end.

Our extended church family welcomed us amongst them the Sunday following Matt's death. It was a time for mutual grief and we were surrounded by many expressions of love as we shared communion together. Family, friends and strangers rallied to comfort us. In profound pain often a hug or brief word reaches deep inside. Helpful friends had barely finished pasting all the messages we received during Matthew's illness into books and now we were once again inundated with cards, letters, e-mails and poignant children's drawings. We read every message at least once draining every drop of comfort from those precious shared thoughts. As people recollected happy memories, those bittersweet reminders of our son applied a strangely soothing balm to our brokenness. We knew we would preserve all those too in our hearts, that we might ponder them again and again.

This Day In Paradise

This day in Paradise
new feet are treading through
high halls of gold

This day in Paradise
new legs are striding over jewelled fields in which
the diamond
is considered ordinary

This day in Paradise
new eyes have glimpsed the deep fire ready
to flame the stale earth pure

This day in Paradise
new blood, the rose-red juice that gushed at Golgotha
now ripples and races down the pure veins
of a recently arrived beloved

This day in Paradise
a new heart pounds in praise
a new body, shaped by sacrifice

This day in Paradise
the daunting dart of death
has no point
no place
and no meaning

And whilst we mourn and weep
through these human hours
This day in Paradise
the blazing embrace
between Saviour and son, goes on, and on, and on...

Chapter 44

Somehow we survived to the day of the funeral celebration. As we prepared for that most painful afternoon, we kept reminding ourselves that Matthew had graduated to a beautiful place and was safe from all harm, even though we were envious of his presence elsewhere. Prior to the mid-afternoon service people called at the house to squeeze our hands, offer support, or just leave cards or flowers. It was arranged for Mark and me to be accompanied in the car following the hearse by my sister Jackie and our friend Patrick as we were in sore need of constantly available arms to lean on throughout the day.

We requested that no one wore black as we wanted people's clothing to be part of their tribute to Matt's love of colour. I wore a beautiful bright turquoise linen coat, not really protection enough against the chilliness of the day, but it was such a joyful colour and so I wrapped a warm pink scarf several times around my neck to keep out the winter winds. Thankfully, the sun shone brightly against a piercing backdrop of blue, adding to the dreamlike quality of that December afternoon.

We floated through much of what was going on, hearing and seeing but as if through thick wadding, until the hearse arrived at our house bringing its own stark reality. A friend from church had created a flower arrangement for us which draped the pale coffin in soft white. Favourite lilies of the valley intermingled with winter greens and the display was crowned with a single blood red rose in the centre. Other family flowers in the shapes of a pillow and football were placed around the coffin, poignant reminders of a young life cut tragically short.

I stood at our front door biting my lip and desperately holding back tears that threatened to engulf me as Daisy, our friend's seven-year old, and Mattie's special girl, asked if his body was in the box. With superficial fortitude, I told her his earthly body was, but that his spirit was safe with Jesus and we would see him again one day. Tears gushed from her eyes as she tried to walk with dignity back into the house. My heart ached for the pain that a seven year-old would feel and what could be said to ease it. But I did not have answers to my own screaming questions, and felt sorely inadequate to answer anyone else's.

I clung to Mark's arm needing to feel his tangible presence and strength. Just as we were about to leave, Helene gave me a small box saying, "You can't go yet Linny, you're not properly dressed." I opened the box and inside was a gold locket, but no ordinary locket this. It was identical to one Mark had given me shortly after we brought Matt home from hospital but had been lost some weeks before while walking the dogs. I was heartbroken because it held pictures of Mark and Matthew. Engraved on the front was a set of footprints and on the back the words, "When you saw one set of footprints it was then that I carried you," an extract from a famous story that had meant a great deal to me at difficult times in my life. As I opened this new locket tears filled my eyes as I realised it too held precious pictures of my husband and son. My friend had gone to the trouble of tracking down another one for me to treasure. She secured the locket around my neck and we were finally ready to go to church with Mattie for the last time.

The short drive from our house to the church was another extraordinary experience. The four of us chatted about trivia, like the fact that the hearse was a Mercedes limo and how Matt would have approved. As we kept a suitable distance in our car behind, our minds too kept a suitable distance between the reality of the situation and the enclosure we had erected to keep us safe and sane. I felt extremely nervous and scared as this was more uncharted territory and I did not know if we could survive the experience.

Neither of us was prepared for the vast number of cars spilling out from the car park and littering the church lane; I had attended grand weddings with less cars in attendance. We stood shivering nervously in the chilly air as we waited for the coffin to be lifted from the hearse. We were to walk behind Matthew as he was carried into the church. Our vicar, Brian Meardon, was outside to greet us and encourage us with his wonderfully gentle smile and reassuring hug. Seeing him we felt strengthened to go on and clasping each other's hands very tightly we followed the pallbearers carrying the body of our son.

The ancient church was packed with people everywhere and extra seating leading up to the alter and upstairs was also filled to capacity. It was strange to see so many familiar faces spanning Matthew's life, alongside those who had only known him for a short time, and some we did not even know but who had been impacted by his remarkable bravery. For Mark and I it was a healing balm to feel the love that emanated in that place. The atmosphere was one of incredible peace. We felt we had come into a safe harbour and were overwhelmed by how many people had come to pay their respects to our unique son who did not consider he had many friends. A selection of our chosen music had played during everyone's arrival and Matt was carried in accompanied by moving words of a favourite song portraying something of the magnificence of Paradise where he now was.

The coffin was set in place at the front of the church and the gathering was led in Matt's favourite worship songs by Eternity, his youth church's band, which included his close friend Tom on guitar and other much-loved friends. Pictures of Matthew at various ages flashed across a huge video screen as we sat and listened to a special song by Blue from the CD we had played so much for him during the past year. The words mirrored our thoughts that afternoon – one day was too long to wait to hold him and see his smile. It was a time stained with tears, a time of unspeakable pain yet heart-stopping joy. All those who had agreed to read from the Bible and pray did so with such courage and love and we sat enraptured at their honouring tributes.

Mark and I stood up to share some of our exceptional personal memories of a beautiful and courageous young man who changed our lives forever. Unsure as to whether we would be able to survive the ordeal, we had asked friends to stand with us when we took the microphone with our hands trembling, our legs wobbling and our mouths extremely dry. But we need not have worried; we found supernatural strength and ease in the telling of our story.

Following an uplifting and encouraging address by Brian about our eternal lives, we sang our last song and prepared to follow Matthew as he left St Michael's for the last time. Crowds of people joined with us to accompany Matt to his resting place in the churchyard. Looking around at everyone we found comfort in the love and support of hundreds of people, young and old, there to pay their personal respects and to honour a shy young man who didn't like to make a fuss. So many of his friends were there, including classmates and best friends from school, who all looked so grown up in their uniforms; yet the pain on their faces reflected a childlike quality, silently begging a response to their questioning expressions.

It is a strange feeling to watch as a wooden box containing your child's body is lowered into the ground. As Mark and I witnessed the final stage of the journey for Matthew's physical presence we had to keep focusing on the promises of God. Our son's spirit, with no further use for his earthly form, was finally with Jesus. As we placed a single red rose and sunflowers on his coffin we remembered with awe, how many lives he had already touched all around the world.

Tributes to our hero shared with family, friends and strangers:

5th December 2002

Mark writes

I lost my dad seventeen years ago in a car crash. In fact he didn't die straight away; he went in and out of intensive care in a similar way to which Matt did. I cried and cried and prayed during his illness and I prayed some more. But my dad died two months later and I was devastated. I had lost my father, my main man, the one I went to in times of trouble, for advice on relationships, finances or just to talk. He was my best friend. I was truly blessed to have a dad like that.

But God had let him die. Why? I did not have a relationship with God then and what little faith I did have left me completely. God hadn't saved my dad so there couldn't be a God could there? I didn't find out the answer then. I just felt aching loss.

Then God gave me Mattie and the opposite of that loss happened. When Matt was born I was given joy again. And boy what joy! I was such a proud father. He was everything I had wanted and I tried to be all a son could wish for in a father. I hope I was. Mattie was the reason I am now able to know God as my heavenly Father and Jesus as my friend.

Mattie grew up into a lovely young man, a little of me and a little of Lyn in him. He was a pretty baby and a handsome boy with the most beautiful blue eyes and ready smile.

He was loving and caring, with a fantastic sense of humour and contagious laugh. Like his buddies he loved the usual things like watching 'Friends' and 'Toy Story'; but what few people knew about him is that he loved programmes like 'Dad's Army', 'Porridge' and 'Last of the Summer Wine'. Entertainment without nasty stuff in it, just good old-fashioned harmless humour. He loved it when we just sat and watched television or films together.

Matt didn't like scary movies or rollercoasters; he would far rather just be with a friend playing simple make-believe games. He loved it when we played hide-and-seek and we always revelled in the excitement of finding one another and having a hug and tickle before the next one's turn. That's what made his day happy.

He loved company, ours or his friends, he loved being with so many of you guys. Thank you mums, dads and friends for all the sleepovers, trips to the park, movies you watched with him, teas he had with you. Thank you for sitting next to him at school, even when you may not have wanted to. Thank you.

Like me, Matt had a passion for cars and we would often disappear down the auctions together much to Lyn's frustration! From an early age, he could name a car make and model from quite a distance away. Mattie loved swimming; it was his strongest sport and most favourite outing. He would long for summer when we would jump into his Nan's outdoor pool together even if we had to crack the ice first. He wasn't bothered about the temperature and enjoyed it so much.

He had a soft side to his character, perhaps too soft I thought sometimes. He would feel people's hurts easily; he didn't like to see anyone upset and would try to protect them if he could. He would always take people under his wing. He had strong views about some things and would often defend people in what he believed to be right, even if that meant clashing with Lyn and me.

He was a totally unique individual. Exciting and fun to be with. But most of all 'cool'. Matt would keep things to himself rather than worry anyone; he was quite a private chap. He would never tell tales and often took the blame for something he hadn't done rather than blame anyone else. His mates were his mates, they were very special, worthy of the loyalty he gave them.

His imagination was vivid and unique as was his ability to remember detail, including drawing a picture from *memory to making a golf bag from pieces of cardboard, with no detail left out.*

Touching words from one of the many cards we received this week were:
"Those we loved and have lost are waiting for us in a place without parting where we'll never have to say goodbye again". Mattie was all a dad could hope for in a son, to me he was perfect. We were best mates and the wait will be far too long to see him again but I know that we will hug in our special way when we find each other again. Look after my boy for me Jesus. God bless you Mattie, until eternity, my son. And don't worry, I know where you are, so I'll find you.

From a mother's heart:
I make no apologies for being completely biased when I talk about our son. Matthew was, and is, simply the best!

From the moment we knew I was pregnant, he was the most wanted and loved baby. So beautiful, strangers were always congratulating us on our pretty girl! He eventually grew into his big expressive blue eyes and in health and sickness, framed by his striking eyebrows, even when he couldn't talk, they spoke volumes. I never remember him being sick or crying unnecessarily as a baby. He was always happy, though as he grew so did his sense of adventure and we've had to make numerous adjustments to DIY ventures and decorating. But, as I said, I make no apologies for my biased memories.

He was extremely gifted artistically and no palette was out of bounds as he and a young friend once kissed every surface in our bedroom with felt-tip pens. His school artwork did not always adorn the classroom walls, but every brush and pencil stroke he created is indelibly printed on the walls of my heart, every clay model replicated in the recesses of my mind to ponder over at will.

Matt loved colours – he used them, wore them and lived his life in full technicolor. Without him our world seems drab and grey. Everything appears out of focus, like I'm trying to see things without my glasses. I saw so much beautiful detail through his eyes. Now I can only see in monochrome.

He loved music having a good ear for rhythmic, soulful stuff. Rap was cool but he was fussy; it had to be 'class' as he called it. He was always singing and had the ability to quickly memorise all the words to songs correctly. It irked him and me that Mark never displayed that same gift. Every time Mark sings it sounds like country and western and all the songs sound the same. As a captive audience Matthew patiently endured his dad's guitar practice sessions during his illness, but was gracious enough to keep his face totally expressionless, which was more than I could achieve.

A very sociable chap our Mattie. He loved being with people. As an only child his biggest wish in life was longed-for brothers and sisters, and his friends were precious to him. Many of his mates have known him since infancy. We were seldom able to consider holidays, outings or even evenings and weekends at home without first arranging a companion for Matt. Everything we did was preceded by, "Who's coming with us?" or "Who's coming round for tea?"

I think his mates, male and female, will agree he was a loyal and caring friend, championing many less-fortunate than himself, in either stature or status. Fortunately his body reflected the size of his heart and he often had a smaller mate tucked under his arm. We nicknamed Mark the Pied Piper, as he was always trailed by Matt and company whatever he did, wherever he went.

I like to think I have been quite a cool mum. I'm not sure if Matt would always agree, but he taught me everything I know about kids and yoof! To be his mum has been the most precious privilege and I am devastated that the practical side has ended prematurely. I will always be his mum. He will always be my Mattie.

His humour brightened every dull day and his vibrant company gave me joy, joy, joy. I have countless, priceless memories to draw upon in dark days that will have to last far longer than the thirteen short years he was here with us. Like the time he applied mascara to his already long, curling lashes. And the day he adventurously repainted our kitchen with black enamel paint!

Matt's bravery and courage throughout his illness inspired Mark and me to carry on. We will never really know how much he suffered and endured, only that he was our reason to get up in the morning and he continues to be our inspiration now — the wind beneath our wings.

As a family we have always verbalised our love for each other. The only maths Matt and I ever enjoyed was when we would go through our ritual numerical declarations of love until one of us could count no more and it would always end with, "Love you infinity Matt"..."Love you infinity and beyond Mum."

Matthew was a great mimic and he could always render me helpless with laughter with his impersonations. Buzz Lightyear remains one of my special favourites. Matthew is my darling boy, my Buzz, my hero.

Now he has gone ahead to be with his hero, Jesus, the only one who could carry him home. One second is too long without you here Mattie, our loss is heaven's gain, as they say. We must wait to be with you for eternity and forever. Until we meet again my precious hero, I love you, infinity and beyond.

We'd like to express our thanks and love for everyone here today and those who couldn't make it, for carrying Matthew in their hearts especially for these last nineteen months. Please share any memories you have of Matt with us. He is a multifaceted jewel and though we have only been privileged to observe some aspects of his worth, I know there are countless other brilliant reflections of his beauty just waiting to be told.

Chapter 45

Not knowing what we should do after the service that afternoon, we only knew that we could not spend the evening on our own in the house surrounded by the deafening silence. We impulsively decided to join friends for a meal at a local pub. Not an obvious choice, you may think, but somehow the normality of life there helped us begin to deal with the awkwardness we felt without Matthew to care for. We will be forever grateful to a lovely waitress who, without knowing anything of our situation, was kind and considerate throughout our meal and contributed just the right amount of small talk to make us feel at ease.

With uncharacteristic fortitude, Mark and I had planned to travel to our prospective new home in France the following day to see the house we had bought and decide whether we had the strength to undertake the planned move without our beloved son. The timing may seem odd but we couldn't think of anything that demanded our urgent attention or physical presence in England and it provided a welcome diversion from facing the reality of our situation. By then we were legally obliged to purchase the property or forfeit a substantial deposit and lose considerable savings on the currency exchange, so we had some important decisions to make.

It seemed we had been cruelly left holding an isolated page of the complex map that was our lives. We could only see our insignificant little page, with no signposts to the broader perspective and little understanding of the paths we travelled and frankly I didn't much care. My pain was my whole being and as emotions overflowed without warning we frequently cried as we mourned the finality and loneliness of life without our third musketeer. We had always been overjoyed with the privilege of being Matt's parents. Now without him and starved of his constant presence and special smile, joy seemed little more than a speck on the horizon. We huddled close to each other and kept praying that God would keep us safely in the shadow of His wings.

Everything felt abnormal without Matt, especially going to France, as all our plans to be there had centred around him. The flight was the first we had taken together without him since his birth and everything we did seemed to scream out our desperation. Like automatons, we hired a car and travelled the hour north from Bordeaux. It was lunchtime as we drove in through the gates welcomed by the owners. They had arranged for us to stay in the small self-contained accommodation next to the farmhouse – close by, in case we needed company, but with precious privacy if required.

This rendezvous was in stark contrast to the previous ones we had separately undertaken with such expectancy. Then it had been the height of summer, the sun was shining and flowers, scents and hope filled the air. Thousands upon thousands of sunflowers seemed to welcome us with heads upturned. Mattie was alive and showing signs of improvement and we were filled with a sense of things turning out well. Now our worst nightmare had become a reality; our son had not recovered but had gone from us and this world. A friend suggested that for so long, as Matt defied his terminal prognosis, it seemed our lives imitated a coin spinning on its end. As long as it kept spinning, there was a fifty/fifty chance that it would fall on the winning side for us. Now the coin spun no more.

Though the sky was a vivid blue, it was chilly and most of the trees looked sad in their minimal winter garb. Without the sunshine reflecting glorious patterns through the trees and onto the pale stonework of the farmhouse, everything looked rather ordinary. We were welcomed and cared for by our hosts but we still pressed close against each other, fearful to allow anything to touch us in case it uncovered the rawness of the wounds we carried.

Our mood did not lighten as we awoke the following morning. We lay in bed looking up at the wooden beams in our room discussing how on earth we could consider making this enormous change of life. I think both of us felt we could not now come to France. Matthew, the very reason for our plans, was gone and we lacked enthusiasm for anything. I remained totally motionless for ages barely breathing, not seeing, and finding some peace in the stillness. I was living between my narrow tram lines. It was the only safe place I knew.

There in France we realised we could never have the life back we had before; it was gone forever. Our precious memories of Matthew were all we had. We didn't like the situation but there was nothing we or anyone could do to change it. The finality of that realisation bruised us over and over again every day. My personal barrel of hope was running dangerously close to empty but Mark was pretty amazing to be with. Despite how he felt inside he exuded a strength that inspired me to go on though I felt beaten. He respected every 'why?' and 'what if?' I cried out from my heart and did his best to answer my relentless questions. His calmness encouraged me to cope with my feelings of desperation, panic, anger and guilt and his immovable faith ensured we kept close to God every day, even when I was too weak or didn't want to. I do not know how he managed to give so much of himself to me in those early days. I could only receive, unable to feel I could ever give anything back to sustain him in return.

I cannot recall the exact moment we decided to go ahead with our plans to move. But during those five days we talked a great deal sharing our pain and grief. Detached, we visited ordinary shops and festive markets in nearby towns that heralded a season we did not care to be involved in. Dreamlike, we even agreed to attend a local fund-raising dinner for sick children with our hosts but, relieved when it was over, we scurried back to the safety of our room to cry through the long hours of the night. But something obviously stirred deep within us both there – to transform a vision that had begun months before at the bedside of a brave young boy – into a reality. A vision we believed that boy would want to see realised, a vision close to his heart, to reach out and help others in their pain and offer them love and hope. But were we up to it without his inspiring presence?

As soon as we returned to England we visited Matt's grave. The newly-dug clods of earth that clung to our shoes as we stood there felt as heavy as our hearts. Still, as if in a dream, I was aware of a deeply intense desire to dig down into the earth with my bare hands, clasp Matt's body to me and make everything right once again. I wondered if harbouring those thoughts meant I was losing my sanity. The grave was strewn with sunflowers, a piercing reminder of the summer countryside around the house in France. There were poignant signs of visits from friends and strangers, mementoes of their love, concern and grief. I wanted to scream. The small plaque that bore our son's name seemed so insignificant compared to the gaping hole in our lives; the dates of his birth and death mockingly close, tauntingly unfair.

I stood silently by the graveside wanting to pledge my future to a dream that bore the hallmarks of our unique and beloved son. But the reality was I was broken and only too eager to admit it. I didn't want to pretend that I had it all together. I was in pain and, in a strange kind of way, I didn't want to deaden that pain; it was part of who I would always be now, it kept me close to our son. I didn't feel brave or ready to go on with life no matter what happened. I wasn't through being disappointed with the hand we had already been dealt. It would be some time before I realised hope was still living inside me, that no matter how far I could fall, the everlasting arms of my God could still reach me.

Mark writes:
Standing by Matt's grave the ache I felt in my stomach at such a loss was enough to break the strongest spirit and will to live, but somehow I believed there was a way through and it gave me a glimmer of hope even in the blackness. I determined to put my trust in God and hang on even though I didn't feel like it. I knew I would always miss Matt with every fibre of my being wherever I lived, but standing there at his graveside I decided we'd throw our lot in with France and the vision for the retreat. We would go there, not because we didn't have Mattie, not running away, but because of him, inspired by him and he would always be there with us. I wanted this retreat in France to speak love to a world of pain and suffering.

Take the time to hug your precious children — however old they are — kiss them and listen to them even when you are busy. For only God knows their tomorrows.

Remember nothing just happens. Every person you meet, every word you speak, every decision you make, has already been seen. Make everything count; we are here in this life for such a short time.

As high as the heavens are above the earth
So high are Your ways to mine
Ways so perfect they never fail me
I know You are good all the time
And through the storm yet I will praise You
Despite it all, yet I will sing
Through good or bad yet I will worship
For You remain the same King of Kings
You are the voice of hope
the anchor of my soul
where there seems to be no way
you make it possible
you are the prince of peace
amidst adversity
my lips will shout for joy
to you the most high

Chapter 46

Courageous resolves and fine intentions aside, it was with trepidation that we approached that Christmas season of 2002. Matthew would have celebrated his fourteenth birthday at the end of December and, returning to the house where we had nursed him for so long, we were overcome once again with the enormity of our loss. We had been virtual prisoners in that place, albeit by choice, because Matt needed us and everything we did was for his well-being. But prisoners nonetheless. Stepping back into the cavernous emptiness of our house we took up our chains again, but now they were chains of overwhelming sorrow and loneliness.

The lounge where Mattie spent his last seventeen months on earth stood abandoned and sad. All the paraphernalia accompanying his care had long since been cleared out and the remaining furniture suddenly seemed far too small. We seldom sat in there, preferring instead to snuggle up in the comforting confines of his den next door, although it was a little crowded with the fast-growing puppies. We would often sit to eat at the big table in the kitchen, a rare treat after eating from trays on our laps for so long, but everywhere lacked the illumination of his presence. His bedroom remained practically untouched since that first scary night so long ago and we didn't often feel strong enough to venture in there. Pathetically insignificant tokens of such a hugely important life caused a drowning sense of pain.

Some dear friends recently moved to Barbados, whose children were grown-up, offered us warm hospitality and a timely invitation to visit over Christmas. So we swapped England's wind and rain-swept shores for much sunnier climes. We spent two weeks exposing our pale bodies to the rejuvenating sun, and our battered spirits to the healing balm of that Caribbean island. We witnessed incredible sunrises and sunsets, swam in warm, crystal clear waters and received huge dollops of love to bandage our fractured lives. We slept underneath a floating white mosquito net, we floated in the white foam of a salty sea and we were swept along on tides of peace. For a short respite at least our spirits were washed and our emotions soothed.

Barbados is an actively Christian island and it was a treat for us to celebrate a Christian festival in such a God-centred place. We sang our hearts out in several churches and I have to say that Christmas carols will never be the same again unless accompanied by a steel band. We cruised around shops listening to wonderful music and made many new friends. We were rendered speechless at the vastness of God's creation, lying on the beach as 2003 was heralded in, humbled by our smallness, yet elated as we caught a glimpse of what Matt could see from above our starry ceiling.

God generously gave us both clear visions of where Matthew was, and whilst it didn't appease our overwhelming sense of loss, it comforted us somewhat to know that he was in a far better place, with no pain or fears, and continuously in the presence of his Jesus in Paradise. Diversely, in grand church presentations and intimate meetings with fellow Christians, God reassured us of His love for us and afforded us minute glimpses of His huge, incomprehensible plans. We listened with tears streaming down our faces, as the song that had played as we walked

Matt's earthly body to the churchyard in Warfield, England, was exquisitely performed live at the People's Cathedral in Christchurch, Barbados.

Two-and-a-half weeks after arriving empty and weak to the island, we left uplifted and encouraged, thanks to the wonderful people we met and the amazing sights we saw. Mark bought a colourful oil painting entitled 'The Rapture' by local artist Rodney Arthur, as it gave us both a precious image of where Matt is. Throughout our stay there it was propped against the wall of our white-washed bedroom and upon our return home was given pride of place on the wall opposite our bed. It was the first thing we saw in the morning and the last thing at night and helped convey a sense of peace to our troubled souls. During a breathtaking visit to the north of the island, we saw how the relentless Atlantic had worn huge protruding jagged rocks smooth with time. We hoped the jagged edges of our pain would one day be worn smooth and the precious memories of our son moulded into a thing of beauty that would touch many lives.

Before coming back to England we detoured via Texas and Florida, visiting more friends who graciously offered their home and hearts to us. The weather graced us once more with warm sunshine, piercing blue skies, crisp mornings and unusually gentle temperatures. But finally the time came to face reality once more as we returned to England at the beginning of that new year, aware it was still the same old world but trusting we had glimpsed something of a new perspective.

Painful memories of Matt's suffering came once more to fill my waking thoughts, though longed-for dreams of happier times still eluded my sleep. I was tortured with feelings of guilt that I had failed my son. Failed to recognise that he had become so seriously ill and failed to do everything that could possibly be done to help him get well. Friends and family continually encouraged me by insisting that no parents would have recognised the severity of Matt's illness nor could have done more for his care. But it was cold comfort as I wrestled with my guilt-laden feelings of inadequacy.

I did have one vivid dream at that time. I dreamt that Mark, Matt and I were on the Titanic and there was one space available on the only remaining lifeboat. I heard God ask me who I would choose to go to safe harbour, given no assurance of survival for the remaining two. We both unhesitatingly put Matt in the lifeboat, prepared to take our chances, as long as he was safe. I believe the dream showed me a new perspective: Matt was safe but Mark and I had things to do. On a good day I could see for miles, but my heart still ached for our darling boy and I had no way of knowing just how long it would take for those jagged rocks to be worn smooth.

Some feelings of trauma are better handled through routine and it became an almost daily ritual to bundle the dogs into the back of the car and drive the five minute journey to the church where Matt's grave was. We would park the car and embark on an exhilarating walk of about an hour across fields and along quiet lanes concluding back at the churchyard. During the exercise we talked about anything and everything and inevitably Matthew. Before returning home we would stand by the graveside, united in our loss, yet separated by our unique and single grief. Erstwhile strangers to gardening, we found an odd comfort in tending the narrow grave plot assigned to our son, planting pockets of bright colours amongst the frequent floral tributes laid there to honour and remember him. We had designed and ordered a headstone to replace the tiny plaque that bore his name – something that would loudly declare the precious worth of our son's earthly body resting there.

Joy wasn't something that came bounding up each day ready to overtake us in abundance. We found we had to seek it in new, unfamiliar circumstances and the bad bits in between were about as low as you could go and still be alive. But, with France on the horizon, we set ourselves realistic goals as we began settling our affairs in England and concentrated on selling the house. The practicalities of that and raising the finances to move to France were numerous but we began in earnest that January. The busyness of it all created another buffer between us and our loss. Our grief continued to engulf us on a daily basis but having something positive to focus on helped us to keep going.

During Matthew's illness I had begun studying homeopathy at home and to occupy more of my surplus time, I devoted three days a week to my studies. It was not my ultimate intention to practise professionally, although if I completed the course I would be qualified, but hoped that I might be able to help future visitors to us in France. I also set aside two days each week to work on a book about Matt. I nurtured a burning desire to write everything down that we had learned, along with a driving need to journal everything I could recall about our son. Eventually, we hoped that people could benefit from our experiences. But it proved extremely difficult emotionally as, in possession of hindsight and further knowledge, I often struggled at leisure with decisions we had made in haste.

At that point in time I found myself again questioning God's part in all of our suffering. I could not believe that He had caused Matthew to become ill and die, but He had certainly allowed it all to happen because, as Almighty God, He could have prevented it. So I had to choose to trust God and His promise never to leave us or forsake us. It was a monumental struggle as I reminded myself the world was not fair but God is God and the two should not be confused. In truth I was confused and the only thing I was sure of was that God was big enough to handle all my tears, shouting and anger without being intimidated into giving immediate answers to my questions. I sensed it was the beginning of a journey that would not be quickly completed.

In answer to my angry questions one day "What if we've all got it wrong? What if there is no God? What if it's just a figment of everyone's imagination?" a wise friend asked me one question by way of an answer. He said, "Okay, supposing we have all got it wrong and there really is no God, would you live your life any differently to the way you do now?" My answer, a resounding "No!", surprised me because I felt so disappointed with the tragic turn of events in my life. But something inside, somewhere deep in my little 'knower', instinctively assured me that I hadn't got it all wrong. I remember reading something about grief and that through the process we can choose to look into a mirror or through a window. I kept praying that I would eventually stop seeing the reflection of me and my pain and glimpse the beautiful landscape God wanted to show me and through that landscape get closer to the Creator of Life. Something inside me was not letting me give up all hope, all belief, no matter how bad I felt, no matter what I had endured.

Chapter 47

Mark had generously been granted a further three months unpaid leave by his employers, postponing his return to work until some time in April, so we tried to make full use of that time together to achieve our immediate goals. Unfortunately, although the previous summer had seen a property boom in our area in the South of England, as a nation we were now facing the prospect of involvement in a war in the Middle East and the money markets and everything dependent on them tottered shakily. 'For Sale' signs lingered worryingly outside houses that previously would have been snapped up by buyers within days. We weren't too alarmed at first, with some viewings and until the end of March to complete the sale before making tracks across the Channel.

As the weeks wore on and prospective buyers for our house became an endangered species, it got a little uncomfortable under the collar as we realised time was passing and we were no nearer to achieving this pivotal goal. As I said, we had already paid a deposit on the house in France which we would lose if we backed out, and had used the remainder of Mark's inheritance from his grandmother to secure the necessary euros to complete the deal. It became apparent that if we did not take up that option by the last day of March, the fluctuating exchange rate could mean our proposed venture would cost us considerably more than we had planned, to the tune of seventeen thousand pounds!

I continued to maintain contact with our friends old and new via e-mail and it was one of our precious lifelines. For so long our computer had kept us in touch with many wonderful people throughout the world during Matthew's protracted battle with his illness and we felt we knew them all personally. It was a profound and humbling thing to know that so many people were still rooting for us and praying daily when we often lacked the strength to put one foot in front of the other. Words of encouragement continued to arrive by all forms of communication and it was an exhilarating feeling to know, in those rare moments when you could hold your head up, carry on and glimpse a higher purpose in life, that hundreds of others were cheering you on. It was also reassuring to know that in the darker times, those same people fervently prayed for strength for us.

Faced with the daily paradox of an aching, stifling loss because Matthew was no longer with us to tangibly touch, kiss and see, and the incomparable joy of knowing that he was in Paradise, that far better place, I felt like a child wanting something selfishly yet trying to understand with my finite little mind that not receiving it was indeed the better way. Rationally, I would not wish him back to this world where happiness is a fleeting emotion fraught with uncertainty and life is littered with tragedies. But too often I was irrational, beyond placating and desperately weeping for his return, yearning to see him in the present, and impatient and tired of our arduous chapters in this infinite tapestry of life. Mark and I climbed to new heights of love and appreciation of each other and plumbed new depths of grief, together and in solitude. We were caught between the now and the not yet, and I found it difficult not to stamp my feet and pout my lips in childlike disappointment.

As February sped by and March threatened to overtake

our schedule, we relentlessly clung to the vision for the retreat in our prospective new home. We stood in faith to leave England for France on April 1st 2003 and co-ordinated our plans to do exactly that, beginning with packing up all our household belongings and tentatively booking a removals firm. We began initiating a Trust Fund. Our vision, to honour Matthew's memory, was to offer love and rest to families in similar circumstances to ours, and ambitiously, extend our hospitality to children in hospices who suffered degenerative illnesses as a direct result of the Chernobyl disaster. Feeling very uncertain about our future we had to trust that if we waited we would see the vision become a reality. Trusting and waiting had never been my strong points and were back to test me again.

Using some already donated money we applied to sponsor a child in need. The monthly contributions would go towards the child's schooling and provide small periodical gifts as well as indirectly benefiting the child's family. For some time we had already had the privilege of sponsoring a girl in Bolivia and a boy in Uganda, but this latest commitment was especially for Matt. He had always wanted a younger sister with dark hair and almond-shaped eyes. His prayer was finally answered when we began corresponding with an eight-year-old girl from the Philippines, called Mary Grace, who had no parents and was living with her grandparents and aunt.

Our bubble came dangerously close to being burst as we ticked off the first few days of March. Still with minimal interest from buyers, we had to admit that the chances of raising the necessary capital from the sale of our house in time to take advantage of our best laid plans, looked unlikely. Mark and I spent two whole days earnestly discussing our remaining possibilities and praying. Frankly the outlook was bleak. Then on a rush of inspiration, Mark declared that he wanted to try to raise the money without first selling our house in England. We had some assets and possessions that could be sold and he asked for my agreement to increase our British mortgage and perhaps borrow the balance from anyone who had any spare cash just lying around waiting to be used for last minute ventures such as ours! I gave consent, hoping against hope, but feeling far from assured that it could be accomplished in time, however diligently Mark worked.

Rather bizarrely that March, our local education authority leafleted our area with details of free tuition in Beginners French. It was a course that would run for four weeks initially to see how much interest it would generate. Although unable to avail ourselves of all four weeks if our prospective dates for France materialised, we decided it was too good an opportunity to pass up and enrolled at our local adult learning centre, within minutes walking distance from home, for the two free hours of French lessons each Tuesday.

In a bid to raise the necessary cash, Mark contacted a helpful financial advisor who had recorded our wills just before Matt became sick. He applied for a remortgage on our English house with only slightly increased repayments and no penalty for early redemption, which of course was what we planned to do as soon as we had sold, which surely couldn't take that much longer we assured ourselves. Unfortunately, even with those extra funds, offering some timeshares for sale and selling many items surplus to our requirements, we were still ridiculously short of the necessary funds. That left people we knew who had plenty of spare cash sitting around in accessible accounts just waiting to be invested in a good cause.

There weren't too many of those – well none actually. Well one, as it turned out: Mark's mum. She too had been left some money by her mother at the same time as Mark. It was an exceedingly long shot, because if she did loan us the total money we still required, it would leave her with no savings and as a single lady in her seventies, that was quite a vulnerable position. But desperate needs require desperate measures and so Mark approached her with our request, explaining that as soon as the house in England was sold we would repay her generous loan. We felt fairly confident we could do that sooner rather than later but less confident about the prospect of Mark's need to return to full-time work to support us in the interim.

With only three weeks to clinch all the deals, transfer money to another country and leave our homeland lock, stock and barrel, it didn't really seem a viable proposition, but nonetheless Mark gave the project his all and beavered away attempting to achieve mission impossible. We continued to pack up the house to the amazement of ourselves and the bewilderment of everyone else. Days slipped away like sand in a timer, I kept packing and Mark lived life with a telephone attached to his ear. I secretly wondered how I would feel being unable to visit my son's earthly grave frequently but prayed that at least the headstone would be in place before we left. If we left.

Chapter 48

Miraculously quickly we received an encouraging indication that things might come together as Mark's mother promised to lend us a rather large sum of money. Next, with comparable speed, we received the offer of an increased mortgage on our existing house. Thanks to our advisor, it was extremely competitive and within our means as long as Mark went back to work fairly soon. Finally, after much bargaining, our timeshares sadly went under the hammer for much less than we knew they were worth, but as it was unlikely we would revisit those places without Matthew we decided they had outrun their usefulness. The sale of our personal possessions didn't meet our expectations and we subsequently ended up giving much away to keep down the costs of removals. What mattered now was whether all the money could be in the right places by the deadline.

A pivotal day dawned about three weeks into March when we had to stand in faith for all the finances coming together in time and confirm the booking for the removal firm and also book the Channel crossing. It was our intention to drive our car towing our lovely old caravan to France on April 1st, known as April Fool's Day in the United Kingdom! With the dogs to consider, we opted for a tunnel crossing. Simba was notorious for throwing up whilst travelling in cars or at the very least drowning Louis with his drooling and we didn't feel brave enough to risk his sea legs on the ferry. In anticipation, we arranged for some strong medication from the vet for the car journey so that he would sleep during the eight hour journey from the tunnel terminal to our destination.

It became increasingly complicated to cook much at home as more and more of our kitchen items were spirited away into packing cases, courtesy of over-zealous helpers, leaving us acutely aware that, sink or swim, we were committed to this venture and thoroughly fed up with jacket potatoes and salad. As April 1st loomed threateningly on the near horizon, we continued to pray and felt a timely sense of peace about the final outcome, whatever that happened to be.

In order for us to purchase the necessary amount of euros we had secured the previous year, the deadline for all the finances to be in our bank account was lunchtime on March 31st. Tension played a starring role as the minutes ticked by that morning and we witnessed our future hang in the balance of scales beyond our control. The operation bore resemblance to an international monetary thriller of huge proportions. We prayed silently and vocally, together and separately. To be or not to be...that is the question. Finally, around one in the afternoon, we received the phone call confirming that the funds were safely though briefly ensconced in our bank. But before they had chance to earn so much as a reputation of interest, they were expedietly passed on to eager recipients.

Mark and I spun around the kitchen and hugged one another victoriously then cried together in disbelief and apprehension as the enormity of the whole enterprise flooded in. The reality was that in twenty-four hours we would be leaving our homeland and embarking on an undertaking we knew little about, for which we had no training and with what suddenly seemed like rapidly diminishing courage.

For the remainder of the day, we frantically continued packing everything into any available box, desperately aware the removal van would be arriving early in the morning – and the few remaining unpacked belongings were doing a good impersonation of multiplying many times all over the house. The dogs knew intuitively something was up but not being sure what, decided the safest course of action was to remain under our feet all the time. The tension in the air was fed by a mixture of trepidation at the prospect of the unknown adventure before us and forlorn sadness that we should still be continuing along this path without the one person for whom we had dreamed this dream.

That night we went to bed for the last time in our room directly above the empty space where our son's special bed had stood for so long, but sleep was elusive as we silently recalled our own precious memories of the past two years. Times stained dark with tears of suffering and pain and briefly colourwashed with sunshine colours of joy. I was suddenly terrified at the prospect of leaving England, Matthew's England, where he had been born into this world and where his earthly body was buried. We had visited the grave that day not knowing when we would next be there and were rewarded with a view of his headstone, finally in place and proudly displaying his beautiful name. We stood transfixed, unable once more to grasp the finality of recent events as we read the words that reflected so much and yet so little of our lives.

Matthew Leitch
1988-2002
With Jesus in Paradise
Until we meet again
love you
Infinity and Beyond
Mum and Dad

I think for the first time in my life I truly realised that I did not belong permanently on this earth and suddenly my heart longed to go home.

Chapter 49

The removal men arrived promptly the following morning. Our continual busyness kept painful innermost thoughts at bay as we oversaw everything being packed into the van and prepared our own little wagon train for the independent crossing that evening. Friends and family had been visiting for many days to say their goodbyes and offer their prayerful support and that day was no exception and in front of others we displayed an assurance we certainly didn't feel. If it had not been for the pressing urgency of the tasks in hand, I am not sure we could not have survived the feelings of emptiness, loss and uncertainty that we both experienced.

Our Channel crossing was booked for six that evening, though fortunately it was flexible and we could turn up and go almost anytime that day as long as there were spaces. It was just as well since everything took three times as long to complete, tempers became more than a little fraught as we worked under extreme pressures and we eventually left the house at roughly the time we should have been boarding the Channel tunnel train. We administered some of the sedative to Simba who flopped around in the boot of the car like some freshly darted lion, careening into Louis, who was only too happy to lie down and sleep anywhere, anytime. Eventually Simba joined his mate in a deep slumber.

Finally, it just remained for us to take another look around the empty sterile rooms that had been a home and hospice for three weary travellers, before locking the front door for the last time. It was a peculiar feeling driving away, not only because we were leaving our home for another country and another life, but we were leaving a huge part of who we were in a small corner of the English countryside. One chapter of our journey was closing, but there was still the matter of the remainder of the book. Would it be a best seller or would it gather dust in some inconspicuous backwater of a foreign land?

As if to urge us onwards, sleeting rain and blustery winds persisted for much of our journey to the coast at Dover as did heavy snoring from one heavily drugged dog and one natural sleep enthusiast. Mark and I chatted about insignificant things interspersed with reminiscent silences until we reached the tunnel check-in. We drove onboard almost immediately and had only a short wait before the announcement informed us that we were departing from England. Exhausted we leaned back in our seats, closed our eyes and held hands for the short half-hour journey. The dogs slept on, unaware they were being dognapped to begin another life far from their old familiar haunts.

Once in France, we had arranged to drive for about an hour-and-a-half to a prearranged campsite where we had booked to stay overnight intending to make an early start, rested and refreshed, the following morning. Although it was late and the darkness prevented us from seeing much of the surrounding countryside, I felt an eerie sadness as we passed through the area of Picardy and the Somme. I thought about the many young lives sacrificed there in two world wars and all the mothers who had lost their sons and my heart ached with a grief even beyond my own.

Finally, we arrived at our temporary destination at the end of an extremely long day and I was overjoyed to open the door of the caravan and discover Mark had already prepared the bed. The prospect of snuggling inside, warmed my otherwise chilled spirits. We quickly stabilised the van as the two sleeping beauties awoke momentarily from their deep slumber to water the trees outside and head eagerly for our inviting-looking bed, until we once more explained the pecking order: the bed was reserved for us and they would be reclining, gratefully, on the floor. It wasn't a popular decision, but it was after midnight and, in no mood to negotiate, we promptly fell into a deep sleep almost as soon as our tired heads touched the pillows.

Morning arrived too soon! We were woken by big wet noses nudging our hands as Simba and Louis informed us they needed to leave the caravan. As they went out to explore, the cold air rushed in reminding us that we had no electricity, no heating and no provisions for breakfast. After a makeshift wash and tidy up, we watered the dogs and administered more tranquillisers for the remaining epic journey and set off in a southerly direction towards the Charente Maritime in south west France.

Most of the morning's journey was along clearly signposted motorway so my limited navigational skills were barely tested until we approached the outskirts of Paris. From bitter experience we knew the city was notorious for swallowing up tourists and incarcerating them in the depths of its complicated ring roads, refusing to spew them out for hours. We proceeded slowly and with extreme caution, not wishing to lose our way and rather miraculously managed to circumvent the busy city without straying onto the wrong road. Feeling more than a little pleased with my map-reading achievements, and of course Mark's adequate driving skills, we buoyantly found ourselves beyond Paris heading south.

At that point I foolishly began to combine map reading with sightseeing – not a recommended diversion for someone with a limited sense of direction. Engrossed in studying the map I remarked how closely we would bypass Versailles and how, in all my previous trips to France, I had never had the opportunity to visit the famous palace. I can't exactly remember at what point we strayed off our intended route, but within a very short space of time, we were close enough to the walls of that selfsame palace to describe the brickwork in glorious architectural detail! To navigate our way out of that city's labyrinth of similar-looking avenues, whilst towing and reversing a caravan, threatened to be the match to the bonfire but as the conversation in the car warmed up, our somnolent four-legged passengers snoozed on.

After pit stops, mistakes, diversions, intense family discussions and essential rearranging of scrunched-up road maps, we finally bid au revoir to Versailles after what will possibly remain our only visit. Compared to that lengthy delay, the remainder of our journey passed uneventfully. The further south we got the more the skies cleared displaying large uninterrupted expanses of blue as a backdrop to the welcoming sunshine.

So it was in the early evening of April 2nd 2003, we arrived at our 'Promised Land', our Canaan, incredibly just minutes behind the removal van containing all our worldly goods. As we entered through the tall wrought iron gates we were united in our grief and silence, thinking about what might have been. Our dearest beloved Matthew, our third musketeer, the person for whom all of this was planned, was not accompanying us in person as we embarked on our new adventure. We knew he would always be with us in spirit and our faith assured us that we would be reunited with him one day, but for now we had to face the challenge of living in this world without him. For so long we had nurtured the hope of carrying him through those big wooden front doors, of nursing him back to complete health in France, that to actually be there without him was an agonising contrast to our cherished dream. Would we be able to survive there without him, or anywhere for that matter? Only God knew the answer to that question. Only God knew if we would survive the desert of our grief, if Canaan would be our Promised Land and the realisation of a huge dream dreamed because of one uniquely special son. Until we meet again darling Mattie, we love you, infinity and beyond...

Twilight of the transfiguration-joy,
Gleam-faced, pure-eyed, strong-willed, high-hearted boy!
Hardly thy life clear forth from heaven was sent,
Ere it broke out into a smile, and went.
So swift thy growth, so true thy goalward bent,
Thou, child and sage inextricably blent,
Wilt one day teach thy father in some heavenly tent.

from 'Diary of an Old Soul' –
Devotional reflection for December 30th
George MacDonald
1824-1905